The Cooperative Family

The Cooperative Family

How Ridding Ourselves of Competitive Goals Helps Us Flourish

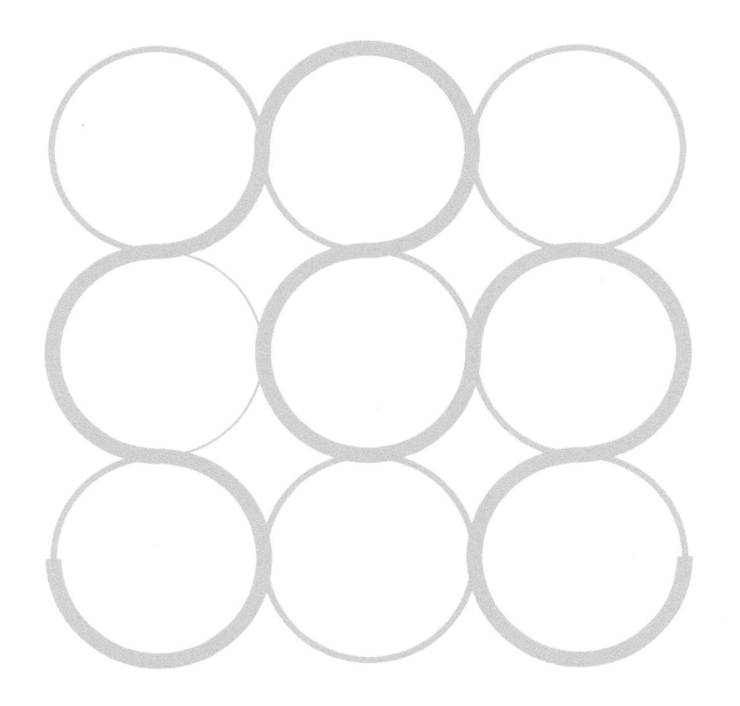

Calvin D. Armerding

Henosis Press, Publisher - Travelers Rest, SC

Published in 2021 by
Henosis Press, Publisher
Travelers Rest, South Carolina 29690

First Published by Henosis Press in 2021

PUBLICATION DATA
Name: Calvin, Armerding, author.
Title: The Cooperative Family
Description: Henosis Press, Travelers Rest, South Carolina, 2021
Originally published: Travelers Rest
Identifiers: ISBN 978-1-7365795-0-3
PSY04100: Psychology / Psychotherapy / Couples & Family Therapy
FAM013000: Family & Relationships / Conflict Resolution
FAM052000: Family & Relationships / Dysfunctional Families

First Printing 2021
Printed in the United States of America

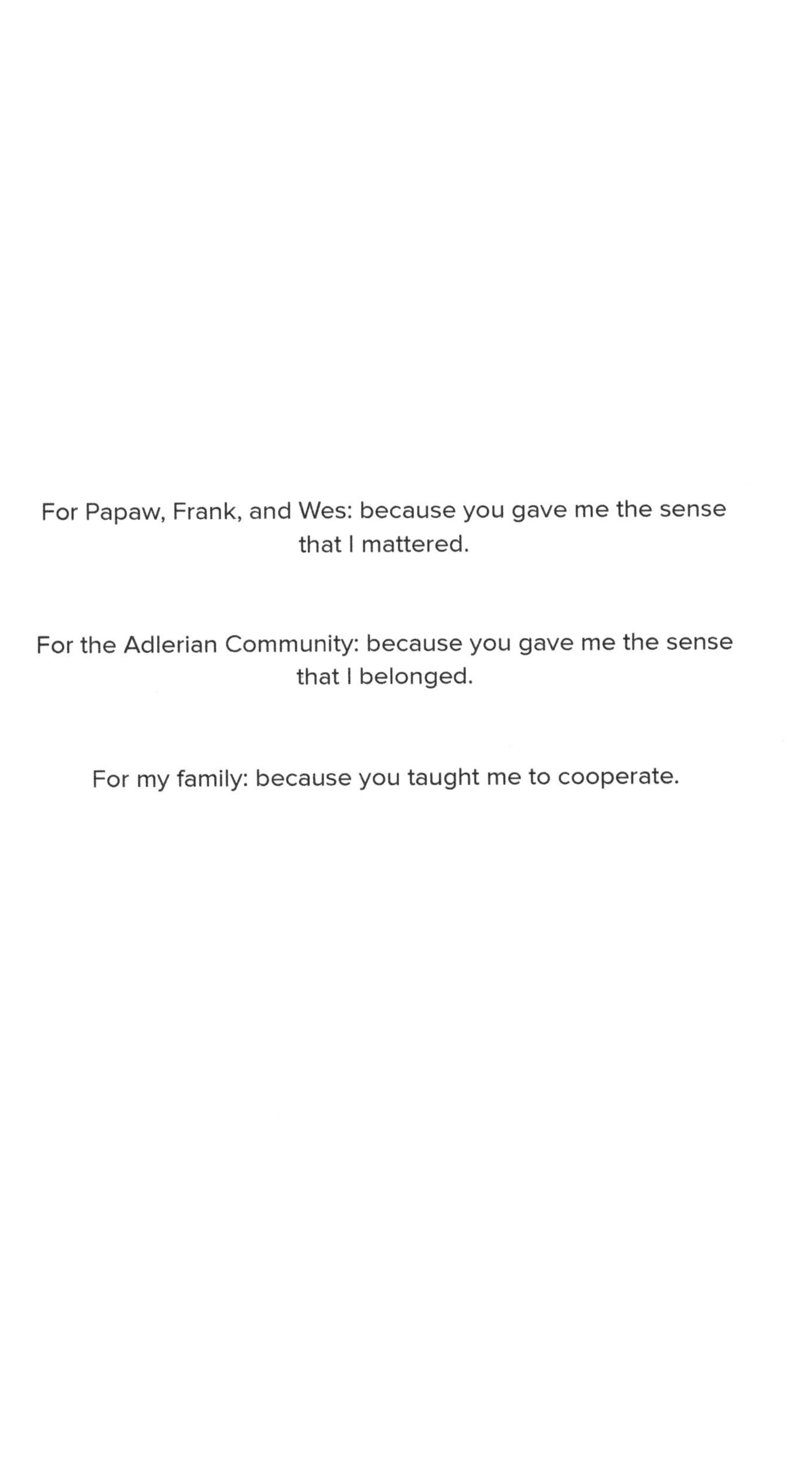

For Papaw, Frank, and Wes: because you gave me the sense that I mattered.

For the Adlerian Community: because you gave me the sense that I belonged.

For my family: because you taught me to cooperate.

Contents

Prologue

As you begin this book, take a moment to look around you and take in your surroundings. Perhaps you are in a bookstore, your home, your office, a favorite coffee shop. Maybe you have a physical copy in hand, or you've downloaded it onto a tablet that you've carried onto an airplane. No matter what situation or location, take a moment to consider the grandeur of human cooperation.

Imagine building the structure surrounding you all by yourself. Even if you are good with your hands, perhaps even a general contractor, where would you get the materials and tools needed to do the job? Maybe you are a real anomaly having the skills needed to fire bricks, mill wood, spin wire, and cast effective tools: you could make do, right?

But what if you had not inherited the knowledge of

these technologies? What if you didn't know what a "wrench" was? What if— in spite of your intelligence, work ethic, strength, talent, and commitment to the project— you simply had no idea how to form and fire clay into uniform, durable stones? Consider the complexity and historical rarity of the plumbing and electric lines behind the drywall. What about where the electrical lines come from (a power plant)? Or where the plumbing lines lead to (a sewer system)?

If you are at the bookstore cheaply skimming the prologue (why buy when you can sample?), look around and consider that you are quite literally surrounded by human attempts to cooperate. Books transmit knowledge and stories, empowering us to learn and understand with awe-inspiring speed and breadth. Just a few hundred years ago, books would have taken months to create— all copied by hand. Consider the efficiency of printing presses, of packaging and delivery systems that not only created the books, but helped them arrive in the room where you are now. Consider how far we have come in order to develop relatively uniform language, and to teach that language to others with unparalleled equity.[1]

The most towering achievements of humankind are the result of an incredibly complex set of cooperative movements. Skyscrapers, political systems, religious movements, technologies, victories over injustice, and great works of art

1 UNESCO (2017) reports that global literacy since 1950 has increased— on average— 5% every decade for the last seven decades.

are simply not possible without cooperation.

Even if we strip away the most extreme or dramatic accomplishments, our survival as a species rests on our ability to cooperate. We are a hairless mammal, lacking strength when compared to other animals our size. We don't have corporeal weapons of defense or attack (e.g., sharp teeth, claws, venom), nor do we exhibit speed or agility when compared to other primates. Yet, we have become the most successful animal species on our planet (perhaps only rivaled by ants and krill, species that don't threaten our existence even while we threaten theirs).

Evolutionary history shows that our intelligence has played a primary role in our dominance, but within the story of human intelligence, another story exists. Intelligence alone has not brought excellence; intelligence has allowed us to cooperate in increasingly complex ways, and that has brought excellence. In fact, intelligence without cooperation has wreaked havoc on our species. Groups of humans have been completely wiped out or prevented from flourishing as we have employed our intelligence to wage war, spread hatred, oppress others, and damage ecosystems essential to our survival. Only when met with cooperative movement does our intelligence serve the species as a whole.

Hunting large game and agricultural cultivation, both highly cooperative tasks, enhanced humanity's ability to develop local communities. Local communities breed culture. Culture breeds law, technology, and religion, provided— of course— that cooperation continues. Cooperation between cultures breeds improved laws, technology, and growth in our understanding of what is significant and meaningful.

This is not, of course, always the cheery-and-delightful path that human history takes. Along with cooperation, our species also regularly engages in competition.

Tribes competed for the grounds on which plants were farmed or large game hunted, and these competitions resulted in the destruction of lives, families, and— in extreme cases— cultures. Cultures don't always cooperate. They can insist upon an inflexible set of laws that they impose on others with violence or threats, destroy technology and knowledge that poses a threat to their way of life, and forcefully limit understanding of what is meaningful and significant.

This is not to say that competition always produces negative outcomes. Civil rights leaders insisted upon their conception of justice, even if it meant disrupting the lives of others who carried with them a different conception of justice. Competition within free market systems generally leads to improved quality of products and services at a lower price for consumers. The non-violent battle between sports teams allows for quality entertainment for spectators as well as fun for the participants.

However, what conspicuously looms behind all of this "positive" competition is a set of cooperative goals. Civil rights leaders provided all Americans— white and non-white— with a more just and fair society. Free market competition helps society at-large through processes of innovation and price-management. Sports competitors entertain spectators and a give a sense of belonging to something bigger than themselves,[2] while simultaneously engaging in cooperative effort on the court/field. Even athletes who play so-called "individual" sports like tennis report the significant contributions of their coaches and trainers.

Many have preceded me in my observation of the importance of cooperation. But, the relative absence of cooperative efforts continue to plague individuals, schools, families, marriages, communities of worship, businesses, cultures, and nations. At a time in which division, contempt, loneliness, and derision are all-too-accurate descriptors of our cultural zeitgeist, it is crucial to remind ourselves of the power of cooperation and the dangers of competition.

This book is an attempt to start the necessary conversations and contemplations that may help us as individuals, families, and larger communities to— forgive the melodrama— be more human by becoming more cooperative.

Our survival as individuals, communities, and as a species has always rested on our ability and willingness to cooperate. It is well within us to cooperate, but our ability does not guarantee action. This book is meant to stir us up out of mere ability into cooperative movement for the sake of ourselves, our families, our communities, and our species.

---

2 For me, the Florida Gator Nation. Go Gators!

I

Striving...But for What?

When I was in seventh grade, my P.E. class focused on team sports. In the fall, we had cycled through basketball, soccer, and a sport invented by some of the P.E. faculty called "speed-ball." Swimming class had dominated the winter, as my school had an indoor swimming complex that got us out of the cold weather. But when spring arrived, it was time to engage in that great American pastime: baseball.

My parents— although generally encouraging of my athletic ambitions— had not allowed me to play Little League baseball. In my hometown, once you moved up from tee-ball to baseball, you were required to attend three practices a week and several games every weekend. My family tolerated the youth soccer schedule: one practice every Wednesday afternoon, one game on Saturday morning. But my parents weren't up to the busyness of baseball— I don't blame them.

The cost of this choice, unfortunately, was that eventually I became a seventh grader who couldn't play ball. I desperately cared about how I was perceived by others, especially a few of the girls in my class. All the rest of the boys had played Little League. When they threw the ball, it flew straight and never seemed to fall from the pull of gravity. Their gloves snatched the ball out of the air without effort. Their bat swings were fast, strong, and clean.

I, on the other hand, threw the ball like a five-pound shot. In the few rare moments when I caught the ball, my glove never seemed to have a good hold on it. When at bat, I struck out repeatedly, even when following the instructions of my P.E. instructor: "Watch the ball." "Follow through." "Choke up on the bat a bit."

Nothing seemed to work.

In a last ditch effort to still be seen as something resembling an athlete, I volunteered to pitch an inning for my team. I thought to myself "I might not be able to do anything else very well, but I bet I can just throw it from the mound to the catcher. Even if the other team hits the pitches, that's just part of the game, right?"

Predictably, this didn't go very well. I threw ball after ball; no strikes. Eventually the P.E. instructor— in a moment of merciful kindness— put his hand on my shoulder and suggested "Why don't we give someone else a try?"

I walked away from the mound— to right field, I'm certain— feeling embarrassed and discouraged. Immediately what became clear to me is that I was— undeniably— *inferior.* I looked at the other 13 year olds around me, knowing that they were— in a word— *superior.*

"Superior."

This word can conjure up feelings of disdain, fear,

frustration, and anger, particularly when we consider the ways in which the word "superior" has appeared in our lives and history. The word might remind us of Adolf Hitler and his vision of a "superior" race, or of contact with white supremacist rhetoric invoking similar ideas about race and culture. We might remember from our personal lives moments where we fearfully huddled in the shadow of a "Superior": a domineering boss, a chest-puffing bully, a know-it-all student, or an authoritarian parent. "Superiority" is a word that captures a whole host of oppressive ideologies, personalities, and interpersonal practices.

It is unfortunate that such connotations dominate our thoughts. While the word undoubtedly implies a dominance hierarchy, what we can miss in all of our connotations is that "superior" can also refer to *excellence*. While there was a dominance hierarchy during that fateful seventh grade baseball game that left me painfully aware of the inferiority of my skill, their superiority was rooted in excellence, not oppression. Their technique was superior. Their swings were superior. Their knowledge of whether to throw to first or second after fielding a ground ball was superior.

Alfred Adler, a 20th century psychiatrist and theorist, made the observation that human beings are constantly oriented towards inferiority-superiority dynamics. In Adler's view, humans are constantly becoming aware of ways in which they are smaller, less capable, less talented, less favored, less safe, less...(fill in the blank).

The baseball game wasn't the first time I had felt inferior. I am a second-born son, meaning that at the time of my birth, my brother was bigger, stronger, more knowledgeable, and better able to communicate with others. He also had a two-year head start in winning the affections of my parents, which he was doing quite effectively. He had already laid claim to the roles of "good child" and "easy child," roles that were never available to me. From the first moments of my life— none of which I remember explicitly— I was undoubtedly aware of my inferiority in relation to my brother.

This is not to say, however, that *my* inferiority feelings were the only ones present in the household at the time. If we consider my brother's experience of my arrival in the family, we would see that he too possessed these feelings.

When I was born, my parents seemed to suddenly be less interested in him, in spite of all his hard work to please them. Family attention and focus was always on the new baby, who— it appeared— could do no wrong. When he screamed, he didn't always (or even frequently) get what he wanted. I, on the other hand, could scream for only a few seconds before both parents immediately jumped into action to attend to my every need. I was constantly being photographed and fawned-over by visitors and extended family; he, the older brother, couldn't compete with this new squirmy bundle.

Adler's observation of the ubiquity of inferiority feelings is demonstrated, even within a "normal" family event (the birth of a new child), both for the new baby and the older sibling. Imagine how easily we could identify these feelings in moments of insult, trauma, pain, embarrassment, or shame, which are— sadly— also ubiquitous human experiences.

Adler (1938) observes more than just inferiority feelings themselves; he observes humanity's response to them. He writes: "To be human is to possess feelings of inferiority *which constantly presses towards its own conquest*" (p. 73). Feelings of inferiority do not end in themselves; they produce and compel movement *away* from the feelings.

Adler calls this movement "striving for superiority." When we notice our inferiorities, we strive to make up for this by achieving excellence (or— equivalently— "superiority"). Adler, an ophthalmologist by trade, noticed that his patients with "organ inferiorities"[3] regularly compensated for these difficulties by becoming prodigious in some other skill. Many physicians and educators have noticed this same trend.

Human inferiorities are not only organic; they are often psychosocial, as illustrated above in my description of myself and my brother at the time of my birth. As a second-born, I wasn't just physically smaller: I was also disentitled to the position of Good Child and Easy Child. My brother wasn't handicapped, but he was abruptly denied an exclusive right to adult attention.

Just as our inferiority feelings can be psychosocial, so our compensations/strivings are often psychosocial. I made up for my smaller stature and chronological age by being "more tough" than my brother.[4] My brother made up for being outshined by the baby by doubling-down on his roles "the Good Child, turning him into a delightful goody-two-shoes.

---

3 E.g., blindness, near-sightedness, physical handicaps, etc.
4 More accurately: 'Meaner."

At any given moment, human beings are in the act of moving away from their feelings of inferiority and striving towards a feeling of superiority. This always involves moving towards excellence of some kind, though "excellence" can take on many forms.

Being a child who is exceptionally mean is, without question, a form of excellence. Being mean afforded me many victories: wrestling matches, one-on-one basketball games, and arguments. These victories were very real; whether they were "good" is another question.

My undergraduate professor Dr. Paul Rasmussen used to say that human beings always want to feel "Better"; "Better is *always* better, but better is *not always good*." The same is true about the excellence for which we strive in response to our inferiority feelings: excellence is *always* excellence, but excellence is *not* always good.

Hitler's army was well-trained. The class know-it-all is well-studied and knowledgeable. The bully is not only strong and physically powerful, but also wise in the ways of human motivation and function.[5] In these examples, the excellence is undeniable; the *goodness* is easily deniable.

This begs an important question: if our feelings of inferiority and consequent strivings for superiority are unavoidable, how are we to tell the difference between "good" and "bad" striving?

5 An effective bully knows what to do and say to get others to cough up the proverbial "lunch money."

My answer is this: *cooperative striving leads to human flourishing, while competitive striving inhibits it.*

It is important to briefly observe that cooperation and competition are not mutually exclusive, even within a single movement. We can cooperate while serving a competitive goal. A businessperson can make a cooperative agreement with another business in order to crush a rival. We also can compete while serving a cooperative goal. To compete in the free market requires making a product that is either more affordable or better quality, which will benefit a community of consumers. How then are we to discern whether we are striving in the "right" way?

We can discover the answer quite simply by answering one question: is the cooperation subordinate to the competition, or is the competition subordinate to the cooperation?

The seemingly cooperative businessman making a deal is only engaging in this behavior to achieve a competitive goal: crushing his rival. The seemingly competitive businesswoman who develops a new product or service engages in the behavior to achieve a cooperative goal: to provide less privileged consumers with a high quality product at a lower price.

Striving for superiority is unavoidable. To attempt to root this out of our behavioral patterns would be a fool's errand. However, it is of utmost importance that we learn to distinguish between striving for superiority *over others* (competition) and striving for superiority *with others* (cooperation). Lydia Sicher, a student of Adler's, makes this distinction using the language of *vertical striving* and *horizontal striving.*

Vertical Striving

Vertical striving is characterized by a desire to elevate the self over others. Adlerian psychologist Zivit Abramson (2007) explains: "The vertical...represents a world in which life is like a scale one must climb." An individual or group who is engaged in vertical striving will likely seek to be right by proving another wrong. They will seek to be excellent— in part— by criticizing the flaws in another; they will prove their worth by demonstrating the relative insignificance of others. Even if their vertical striving does not involve putting others down, they will understand their own sense of self-worth and excellence only in comparison to others. "Am I better than ________?"

We might be tempted to identify only the successful as being vertical strivers. In reality, a competitive, vertical style of striving can also lead to failures of all kinds. Abramson notes that those who strive vertically "include those who work hard to climb high and those who avoid climbing altogether to avoid the risk of failing to reach the top." The subtle danger of a competitive goal is that those who are discouraged about "winning" (their ultimate goal), opt for one of three different strategies: *1) quitting, 2) cheating, or 3) playing mistaken games.*

1. Quitting

Imagine, for a moment, that you are an amateur basketball player. You're not a complete novice, as you play several times a week at your local gym. Your teammates and opponents are mostly middle-aged, and generally match your skill level. You arrive, ready to play. You stretch, warm up with a few layups and jump shots, and chat with your play partners.

Now imagine that in through the door walks Lebron James. Six feet, eight inches tall. 250 pounds of pure lean muscle. He has quickness that more than doubles everyone else on the court. Perhaps he signs a few autographs, shakes some hands. Then, he makes it clear that he wants to play.

At first, you're flattered and excited. *You get to play with Lebron James(!)*, one of the best to ever play the game of basketball. You imagine the stories you'll be able to tell your friends, the pictures you can show at your next work party.

Then the game starts.

Play after play, possession after possession, Lebron drives to the hoop and dunks forcefully. Any attempts to defend, steal— even foul!— don't seem to deter him at all. Eventually, everyone involved seems to get bored with the whole thing, even Lebron. Winning, or ever stopping him momentarily, becomes a purely hopeless endeavor. It occurs to everyone on the court— even his own team— that their efforts, skills, and attempts are utterly insignificant in the face of what he brings to the court.

What is likely to happen is that everyone will eventually quit playing. Perhaps they'll just slink off to the sidelines to snap pictures with their phones. Perhaps they'll suggest that Lebron just show off some acrobatic dunks after throwing the ball against the backboard, unguarded. Whatever happens, it's likely that they will quit playing the game, precisely because it's a *hopeless challenge*.[6]

We witness this same tendency in non-human mammals.

Steven Siviy of Gettysburg College studies play behavior in rats. Rats are a deeply social species, and they love to play with one another, commonly in a form of "rat wrestling." Siviy observes that while larger rats usually— and predictably— win these matches, they will also occasionally allow a smaller rat to win. Siviy contends that this behavior occurs because if the larger rat wins every time, the smaller rat will cease to play. Rats, like humans, will quit if they feel that the challenge that they face is hopeless.

Young students often give up on school when they feel that they "aren't smart." Couples call it quits when differences become "irreconcilable." Depressives attempt and— tragically— commit suicide when life appears to be an endless string of opportunities to fail or "make things worse." Quitting is an effective strategy when a competition appears to inevitably end in a loss. Sadly, it is often an unnecessary response, as it ignores the opportunities that cooperation can provide.

If Lebron were willing to cooperate with the amateur

---

6 The retreat from a challenge perceived to be hopeless is, according to Rasmussen (2010), the essence of depression. It might be difficult for us to consider depressive individuals as being competitive, as they appear to be without ambition or motivation towards any goal whatsoever. We should not be fooled, as there is great power in withdrawal: *we can't lose a game that we don't play, and sometimes not losing can feel like winning.*

players and self-handicap for the good of the group, the game would be more fun for everyone. [7] In the same way that the larger rat allows the smaller rat to win the wrestling match, Lebron could agree to only use his left hand and promise to stay out of the paint. He would still dominate the game, but his opponents would be able to take part in the struggle with a sense of significance, all the same. But, they would only enjoy the game— even with the added handicaps— if winning the game (the competitive task) is subordinate to helping the group to exercise and have fun (the cooperative task).

When discouraged students are encouraged to forgo comparisons to "the smart kids" and attend to their own efforts, school-work often improves and unique interests emerge. When couples relent in their pursuit of sole ownership of the "one up" position and attend to the needs of the relationship, irreconcilable differences often become workable again. When the depressed individual ceases to look up to others with jealous envy ("If only things worked well for me like they do for her!") and turn their attention to the daily tasks of living (e.g., get out of bed, take a shower, go to work, be helpful) their risk of ongoing depressive symptoms and suicide plummet. When cooperation is the goal, quitting becomes unnecessary and distasteful.

---

7 It is unreasonable to expect that those who are more capable must always be handicapped in the service of fairness. "Fairness" can be demanded in a competitive spirit: "You are more capable, so now you *must* be handicapped so I don't look so bad." Self-handicapping for the good of the group is very different from members of the group *handicapping another against his or her will in order to gain competitive advantage.*

2. Cheating

Amos Shurr & Ilana Ritov (2016) studied cheating behavior in adults by putting participants through a set of experiments. By having participants play a series of dice games in which they could win a small amount of money, they discovered that being labeled a "Winner" in one game (a way to prime a competitive mindset) increased the likelihood individuals would cheat in a subsequent game. A follow-up study demonstrated that if participants were asked to remember a time when they had won a competition, they were more likely to cheat than participants who were asked to remember a time when they accomplished a goal.

What this research suggests is that individuals who strive vertically (pursuing a competitive goal of superiority *over* others) are more likely to cheat.

Why cheat?

If our ultimate goal is to win by defeating others, and winning seems to be impossible, we will do whatever it takes to serve the ultimate goal, even if it means violating our moral sensibilities. Human beings will not stand to remain in a position of inferiority. If to lose a competition means being inferior and a loss feels inevitable, cheating is— at least in the short run— a way out.

It's only a matter of time before cheaters are found out. Bernie Madoff demonstrated his superiority over others, first with his extravagant wealth, secondly by his ability to outsmart his "investors." But his cheating was found out, and now his name is synonymous with usury and exploitation. He has been publicly shamed in a way that most people would not be able to stomach.

Cooperation prevents any need to cheat, because the flourishing of those around us brings us joy. When life's challenges are a communal endeavor— a group task— the victory of others brings us a sense of confidence and security, even if we don't love losing. If any competition is subordinate to the cooperative goal, cheating becomes a non-option. Cheating helps an individual win, but brings distrust and ruin to a group. Cooperative goals might force us to tolerate a loss, but promotes human flourishing.

3. Playing Mistaken Games

In my work as a counselor, I often consult with parents about their misbehaving children. In our initial session, I always spend most of the time simply *listening* to parents concerns. I listen to communicate care and understanding, but also to discover the *purpose* of their child's misbehavior.

Rudolf Dreikurs (1964) observed that misbehavior generally has one of four purposes:

1. *To gain undue attention from others.*
2. *To claim undue power and/or control over others.*
3. *To exact revenge or "get even."*
4. *To display inadequacy, thereby conscripting others into service or excusing oneself from something unpleasant.*

When I listen well, it rarely takes very long for me to make a good guess about what a misbehaving child is up to. If I make a correct guess, parents or caregivers often sigh in relief. It can be refreshing to have some understanding of their child's behavior that has confounded them for months or even years. However, sometimes they stare back, quite puzzled. For example, I often observe that a child is after undue power/control in a dialogue something like this:

> ***Therapist**: It seems like James really wants the power in the family. He seems to be doing a great job of showing you that no one is the boss of him, that he won't do anything he doesn't want to.*
> ***Mom**: Yes, definitely, that's what he wants. But we are in charge of him, aren't we?*
> ***Therapist**: You tell me.*
> ***Mom**: Well, we're supposed to be, aren't we?*
> ***Therapist**: You don't sound too sure of yourself.*
> ***Dad**: That's because we're not really sure of ourselves. We are definitely the boss of him, but it...it feels like that's not how it works out.*

These parents are in a tough spot. They are not *only* dealing with an obstinate James, but are also confused. Why? Because James is not playing the same game as Mom and Dad.

Mom and Dad want to be in control, yes;[8] but they want to be in control because they love James and want him to be disciplined, well-mannered, and helpful. James, on the

---

8 While it is perfectly natural for humans to crave control, a superordinate goal of control is mistaken. Controlling ourselves is already difficult, and if we orient ourselves towards controlling others, we set ourselves up against others. We will either be effective in our pursuit of control by using manipulation or tyranny, or we will be chronically anxious, angry, and disappointed that others don't do what we want. Both outcomes put us at odds with others.

other hand, simply wants to be in control. He's not playing the child development game; he's playing the "Who-Is-In-Charge" game.

This misalignment causes the parents to feel very *out of control*. James digs in his heels at every turn. They realize that they cannot make James do as they think he should. Their awareness of their own *powerlessness* (inferiority) tragically motivates them to play James' game. They now dig in their heels, struggle to discern which battles are worth picking, and use threats and bribes to gain *control* (superiority).

James continues to win his game because he's willing to go farther in the power struggle. James' parents are kind and loving people. They simply cannot match his ability to insult, criticize, be cruel, yell, and risk the quality—or presence!— of a future relationship.

James, not exactly the poster-child for the ambitious, successful child, is the very embodiment of the competitive goal. Any cooperative efforts that he makes with his parents are subordinate to the competitive goal of showing them "You aren't the boss of me." He plays his competitive game so well that he gets the whole family involved.

I will, in a later chapter, address how to attend to these types of situations in greater detail. However, it is sufficient at this point in time to note that *cooperation is the cure*. Until any power struggles are subordinate to the cooperative goals of family life and child development, no progress will be made in the relationship. James is fundamentally oriented towards superiority *over* his parents, and unfortunately his parents are now fundamentally oriented in gaining superiority *over* James. Rather than playing the *real* game— attending to the demands of life and development— the family opts to play another game: win the battle, to hell with everything else.

It is not uncommon for vertical strivers to play mistaken games. To invoke Dr. Paul Rasmussen, these games always seem "better" to the individual, but they are rarely good. They constantly win victories, but feel more inferior by the minute, precisely because they are losing the *real* game. James will show his parents that he doesn't have to sleep when they want him to by staying up until 3 a.m.; nonetheless, he'll feel like hell in the morning after his measly four and a half hours of sleep, leading to significant disruptions in peer relationships, academic performance, and daily life tasks. James wins an almost infinite number of battles in his mistaken game, but loses the war of life's actual demands.

Horizontal Striving

Vertical striving produces only winners and losers, and even the winners have targets on their back that keep them worried about losing their *next* battle. Life becomes a never-ending series of trials that put us at odds with others. Horizontal striving, contrarily, is concerned with the elevation of a group or community. Abramson (2007) writes "the horizontal...represents a world picture in which life is a cooperative endeavor among equals." Those engaged in horizontal striving will — without question — seek to be excellent, but their measure of excellence will depend on the well-being of their group/community. Horizontal strivers will work hard to make money, but be generous with their wealth and pay their employees

Vertical Striving*

Superiority *Over* Others

**Disclaimer: do not drown others to stay afloat.*

Horizontal Striving

Superiority *With/For* Others

fairly; they will develop their strength and agility, but because they recognize the contribution they can make to a team effort; they will strive for a promotion because of a desire to be in a position of increased influence for the good of the group.

Strategies like quitting, cheating, or mistaken games are simply unnecessary for the individual oriented towards cooperation. Defeats are less frightening because they occur within the safety of a community. When losses occur, nothing ultimate has been lost if the community continues to flourish.

A famous story about Fred Rogers (of "Mr. Rogers' Neighborhood" fame) illustrates the point. Rogers shared: "When I was a boy and I would see scary things in the news, my mother would say to me, 'Look for the helpers. You will always find people who are helping.' " This oft-quoted story has unfortunately been misunderstood as a call to distraction from disaster, a cheap consolation for tragedy. What is missed in this perspective is the emphasis on cooperation.

Rogers' mother was helping little Fred to see: "You're not in this alone." Her message was not a feeble invitation to only pay attention to the "good stuff." When tragedy strikes, blocking out the "bad" might be immediately helpful; in the long-term, Pollyanna naïveté serves no one— especially the community as a whole, as we need to confront problems rather than avoid them. Cooperation allows us to look tragedy in the face, but with confidence as we attend to the well-being of a community, rather than just ourselves.

Failing a ninth-grade math test is terrifying for the student whose ultimate goal is to have the highest GPA at graduation. Failing the same test is undoubtedly unpleasant for a cooperator, but not catastrophic. The goal was never to be better than others, but to master the material. A failing grade can, in fact, be given a more positive meaning: "I have more work to do before I'm able to lend a hand with this skill."

Victories, also, are less destructive to horizontal strivers. While vertical strivers enjoy their victories, they also feel immense pressure to "keep the gravy train rolling." Winning an award feels great because they've elevated themselves above their competitors; it also is terrifying, because they now have a target on their backs as Top Dog. Within competitive movement, victories are bittersweet— heavy on the bitter, light on the sweet.

For horizontal strivers, victories are empowering experiences that compel them to— in turn— empower others. In cooperative movement, a promotion isn't accompanied by worry and fret about heightened competition and pressure. Rather, a promotion is an opportunity to help others in a position of increased influence. An honor like "Valedictorian" puts no pressure on the recipient; it does empower them to voice encouragements at a graduation ceremony, and reflects *actual learning* (rather than just academic results) that will improve their ability to act as a pro-social member of their community.

Conclusion

Human beings are— without exception— moving away from feelings of inferiority and striving for superiority. The only meaningful difference in how we go about it is this: do we strive to be superior *over* others, or do we strive to be superior *with and for* others? It is a question with far-reaching implications for the everyday challenges faced by humanity.

While much could be said about the importance of developing cooperation and horizontal striving in schools, businesses, neighborhoods, places of worship, and political arenas, it is worth recognizing that the *family is our first community*. Within the confines of the family, we learn our strengths and weaknesses, figure out how to solve problems, and determine how to get along with others. Our parents provide for us a prototype of the high end of a competence/dominance hierarchy; our siblings give us prototypes of those parts of the hierarchies within our reach. Family rules— whether overt or covert— serve as prototypes for laws and social norms; our rebellions— whether overt or covert— serve as templates for how to get around them.

If, then, we can learn to develop cooperative goals within our families, it is likely that we will take our horizontal striving out into our community relationships, subordinating any competitive goals to the ultimatum of cooperation. If we only learn to compete, we will likely take our vertical striving out into the world, putting us at odds with those in our community. To regard the skills of cooperative living as "something we'll grow into" or "a nice idea for a later phase of life" is to put ourselves in danger of falling prey to the ways of vertical striving. The time to orient towards cooperation is always now, whatever our phase of life.

2

The Cooperative Family

In my work as a counselor, I've consistently observed that the family of origin often proves to be the most influential factor in the development of my clients, for good and for ill. Early twentieth-century psychologist Alfred Adler believed that most people develop their *Lebenstil* ("lifestyle" or "style of living")[9] by the time that they are five years old. If we accept this premise, we also must accept the idea that our style of life is developed primarily within the context of the family. This also means that how we choose to engage in life as a family has lasting effects not only on the family unit, but for life.

---

9 When Adler writes of the "lifestyle," he is not referring to fashion choices or anything resembling what we might find in a "lifestyle magazine." Rather, a *Lebenstil* is a patterned way of managing the challenges of life that is unique to an individual. While one individual might respond to the challenge of failure by doubling efforts to succeed, another might give up to conserve energy and solicit pity. Yet another individual might find a way to cheat, or to "ride the coattails" of a more successful person. Yet another might lower their expectations for themselves, leading to contentedness or a slovenly approach to living. The possibilities are endless!

The Family's Power to Shape Our Striving

The power of family influence is double-edged. I have witnessed the havoc that has been wreaked upon clients who grew up in abusive or neglectful environments. It is incredibly difficult to make a positive life-meaning out of experiences of chronic abuse, insult, and trauma. Imagine the struggle of remaining hopeful in relationships when early interactions with parents and siblings are overwhelmingly characterized by the message: "You don't matter" or "You're not good enough." Families can hurt in ways that friends and peers cannot.

Contrarily, I have witnessed the healing and restoration that has come from an authentic apology from a parent to a child. I have seen the resilience of adults and children who have secure attachments to caregivers and siblings, even in the midst of abuse, insult, and trauma. I have seen firsthand the power of parenting built on mutual respect, limits, and an untouchable message of "I love you, I am for you, and you matter." Families can heal and empower in ways that friends and peers cannot.

These descriptions of harm and healing are both real and common. That being said, they are the extreme ends of the spectrum. Most people understand that abusive and condemning approaches to parenting and family life are sub-optimal. Most people understand that humility, affirmation, and unconditional love are powerful in bringing forth positive outcomes in families. Nonetheless, most people live in family systems that manifest themselves in between these two extremes.

My own family wasn't rife with insult, beatings, or traumatic experiences. My parents never openly communicated to me "You're not good enough" or "You don't matter." Much to the contrary, I was— by and large— treated with kindness. That said, the family environment that I grew up in created, reinforced, and maintained problematic mindsets and behavior.

Among these problematic mindsets was an ongoing competition that could be titled "Who is right?" While not without its benefits, this competition would result in regular after-dinner "conversations"[10] that would last for hours. Each of us had our own competitive style and strategy. Some of us used emotional appeals. Others set up straw men. In our own ways, we all appealed to logic. When we wanted to bring out the big guns, we would invoke authority from "experts" or— even better— the Bible. Our arguments didn't always get ugly, but they often did.

I don't share this information as a complaint about my family. Rather, I wish to illustrate that the world is not made up of "good" and "bad" families. The vast majority of us live in the in-betweens of well-intended, somewhat civil competition. Cooperation, while it is given regular lip service, is regularly undermined by a competitive atmosphere. We compete for power, for attention, for significance, for control, and for the service and approval of others.

Think, for a moment, about the problems that emerged in your own family environment, or those that

10 "Conversation" is a common euphemism for "argument."

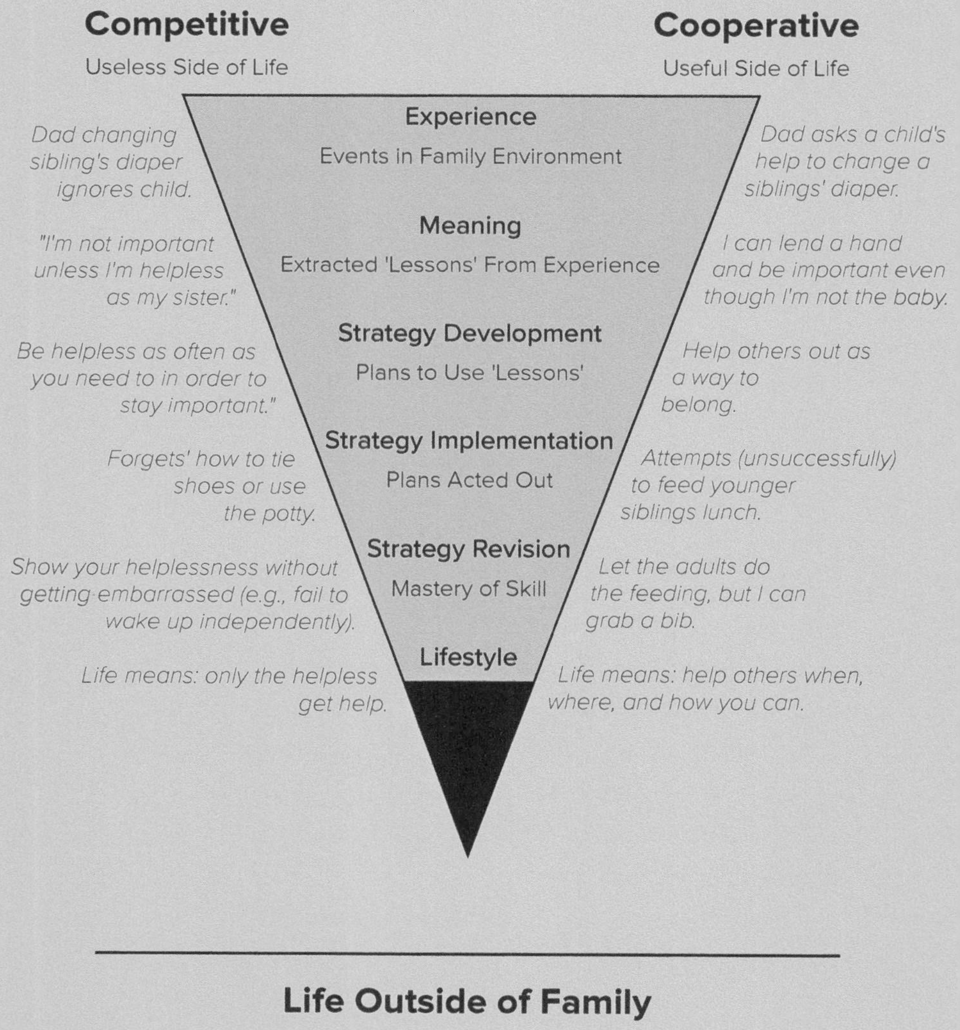

Competitive

Useless Side of Life

Cooperative

Useful Side of Life

Experience

Events in Family Environment

Dad changing sibling's diaper ignores child.

Dad asks a child's help to change a siblings' diaper.

Meaning

Extracted 'Lessons' From Experience

"I'm not important unless I'm helpless as my sister."

I can lend a hand and be important even though I'm not the baby.

Strategy Development

Plans to Use 'Lessons'

Be helpless as often as you need to in order to stay important."

Help others out as a way to belong.

Strategy Implementation

Plans Acted Out

Forgets' how to tie shoes or use the potty.

Attempts (unsuccessfully) to feed younger siblings lunch.

Strategy Revision

Mastery of Skill

Show your helplessness without getting embarrassed (e.g., fail to wake up independently).

Let the adults do the feeding, but I can grab a bib.

Lifestyle

Life means: only the helpless get help.

Life means: help others when, where, and how you can.

Life Outside of Family

currently exist. Take a moment to write a few of them down. Once you have a list (hopefully shorter than longer), consider this: *these problems reveal a lack of cooperative goals and a prevalence of competitive goals.*

Competition (or lack of cooperation) emerges in three different kinds of relationships within families: the marriage relationship, the parent-child relationship, and the sibling relationship(s).[11] The emergent properties of these three relationships determines the outcomes of the family behavior, and whether family members have the opportunity to feel at home, secure, and significant.

11 Intergenerational competition is also on the rise, and while likely an emergent property of competitions between life partners, siblings, and between children and their parents, it deserves special attention. Chapter 6 offers brief observations about our need for improved intergenerational cooperation.

3

Competition & Cooperation in Marriages & Partnerships

Willard and Marguerite Beecher, two students of Alfred Adler, relay a story in their book *The Mark of Cain* about a former client of Adler's who embodied jealous competition. When Adler was informed by a friend that the woman had recently married, he asked the friend: "Against whom?"

Adler's observation that even a marriage can serve our desire to defeat others offers deep insight and honesty about the relational tone of many partnership. Like any other relationship, they can become a battleground with a pronounced "Winner" and "Loser."

Case Study: Chase & Mary

Chase and Mary met late in their junior year of college at a business networking event. Chase was tall and ruddy; Mary was petite and lovely. They had a wonderful first evening together, spending much of the event huddled in a corner making each other laugh. Regular dates followed, and soon after graduation, they got engaged. They agreed to marry a year later, allowing time for them to both secure employment.

At first, everything seemed to be going well. Soon both were employed and earning substantial salaries. (Not unimportantly, Chase made a bit more than Mary, even though their jobs were similar.) Chase got more handsome by the week. Mary's beauty grew at an equal pace. Her engagement ring was bigger than those of all of her friends, and she missed no opportunity to show it off. Chase was engaged to a woman more beautiful than all of his friends' partners, and he also made certain to make a show of his beautiful bride-to-be.

Social media posts about their engagement garnered huge numbers of "likes" and positive comments:

Beautiful! #powercouple

If only we could all have a fiancé (or a ring!) like that!

THIS is how you do engagement. #lifegoals

They secured a beautiful wedding venue through a lucky break: the venue had been booked out two years in advance, but a last-minute cancellation by another couple allowed them to "beat out" the other couples clamoring for a reservation.[12]

Life was good, and the future looked bright.

However, as the wedding got closer and closer, significant problems began to emerge. Chase and Mary couldn't

12 Notice: even reserving a venue for their wedding is seen as an opportunity to defeat others in competition.

agree with one another about the wedding. Chase wanted to wear— with his groomsmen— slim-fitting blue suits with brown shoes. Mary insisted that this was too casual, and that they *simply* must wear black tuxes with bow ties. Mary wanted a live band; Chase observed that this would be three times the cost of a DJ, and felt that money should be spent on a wider variety of hors d'oeuvres at the reception. Chase wanted candles; Mary wanted string lights. Mary wanted roast beef as the main course; Chase wanted steak.

While their social media posts continued to portray the couple as cuddly, flushed, in sync, and overjoyed, their private interactions became increasingly tense and unpleasant. Disagreements escalated into tearful fights and slammed doors. Chase and Mary began to see one another as adversaries.

Chase's competitive tactics involved appeals to logic and numbers. Cost-benefit analyses, practical limitations, and pseudo-political rhetoric were the weapons he used in his attempt to defeat Mary. It was not uncommon to hear Chase accusing Mary of being a "Princess" who was all-too-eager to spend his hard-earned money on things that didn't matter. Spreadsheets were one of his favorite tools, although— notably— Mary didn't really look at them. When she opted out of his trap, he would throw up his hands, storm out of the room, and say "Fine. Why don't you just have the wedding you want? Spend as much as you want. Who cares what I think?"[13]

Mary, on the other hand, utilized emotions and displays of inadequacy as her tactics. Tears, meekness, and claims of injustice were not uncommon. When Chase complained about the finances, she pointed out to him that it would all be affordable if she could just be paid a fair wage: she does the same work for less pay, how was that fair?[14] When Chase brought out the spreadsheets, she would claim that she wasn't "good with numbers; it's all Greek to me!"[15] When Chase became angry and left the room, she would cry and feel terrible, but would also take Chase at his word, and get her way with some decision about the wedding.

At long last— but only a few weeks before the wedding— Chase and Mary agreed to see a counselor about their conflict. The counselor, a friend of Mary's family, was incredibly helpful in that she listened well, understood their perspectives, and normalized their stress level leading up to the wedding. Unfortunately, the counselor encouraged the couple to take a compromise-based approach to making decisions about the wedding, as they "didn't have much time." She had each of them write down five deal-breakers: decisions on which they felt they could not, as individuals, budge. The counselor's hope was that they would each name different deal-breakers, after which they would realize that

13 Translation: "You can win this battle about ganache vs. buttercream icing on the cake, but you'll never win the war, because I'll hold this over your head. I'm the victim now, and that means I have the right to make you feel as guilty as I please whenever I like. Have it your way, but get ready, because I'll punish you for it."
14 Translation: "I've been treated unjustly by my employer, and now it's your job to make up for it. If you don't, you're no good. I have the upper hand."
15 Translation: "I can't understand the numbers, so they can't/won't convince me that you're right."

there was ample room for compromise.

Unfortunately— almost miraculously— they wrote down an identical list: the garb of the groomsmen, the icing on the cake, the music at the reception, whether speeches would be given at the rehearsal dinner or the reception, and whether sparklers or bubbles would be used by the guests at the "send out." Years later, both Chase and Mary would puzzle over why, of all the decisions to be made about the wedding, *these five* were so important to them.

The counselor was totally lost as to how to proceed; this strategy had worked most of the time with couples, who— on rare occasions— might have had one or two items match up. Never all five! What was she to do now? Unfortunately, the counselor identified more closely with Mary's perspective, and encouraged Chase to be "sacrificial" towards his soon-to-be-wife, noting that weddings are "really the territory of women. You have to understand, all women dream about their weddings from the time they are little girls! You may have had these preferences for a while, and that's important of course, but she's wanted these things her whole life."

Chase (understandably) felt ganged-up-on and he informed Mary he would never go back to couples' counseling.[16]

16 Translation: "If I am going to get ganged up on, I won't play the game anymore. You're not going to box me in again."

Nonetheless, Chase took his licks for the good of the relationship. He let Mary win: the groomsmen wore tuxes, they got a live band for the reception, the cake had ganache, speeches were given at the rehearsal dinner, and they left the wedding amidst a sea of sparklers. Mary felt vindicated, and had a new affection for this "amazing man who sacrifices so much for me and the things I hold to be important" (a quote from an abnormally "vulnerable" social media post a week before the wedding).

Chase, who on the surface was basking in the newfound peace between himself and Mary, along with her smiling approval, was unconsciously stewing and plotting his revenge. He began to store up a long record of injustices. He turned into an "extrapolator"[17]: because of how the wedding went, he began to expect Mary to be a frivolous spender, and consequently began crafting— in isolation— strict budgets that he would, over the next few years, enforce with an iron hand. He determined that he would set up a personal bank account, into which he would funnel the "extra" money that he made (i.e., all the difference between his salary and Mary's). "If she's going to be pissed that I make more than her, she'll just have to live with what it would be like if I earned

17 Extrapolation is quite normal. We take the information available to us, and then extend it into the future to increase the predictability of our lives. *What* information we choose to extrapolate says a lot about our willingness—or lack thereof— to cooperate. It's notable that Chase only chooses to extrapolate information that puts Mary in the "one-down" position, rather than her better qualities. This allows Chase to count against Mary faults mistakes that she hasn't even made yet, which is competitively powerful.

the same. I'm not going to bring more to the marriage than she is."

He allowed Mary to get her way almost all the time, but would often punish her for it later with declarations of "I told you so" or "This is why you drive me nuts" when things didn't turn out well. He also began seeing a woman on the side a few years into the marriage, feeling that he was entitled to some comfort and pleasure, since Mary really just wanted to get her way. He made an almost innumerable amount of sacrifices and compromises, but always held them against her in arguments or in private. When Mary finally discovered the affair, he accused her of driving him "straight into her arms" because she was so cold and didn't care about him.

Mary, on the other hand, became more meek, reserved, and tearful by the year. She got almost anything she wanted: her home was filled with beautiful furniture, a late-model car of her choosing was always in the garage, and her wardrobe went through a complete turn-over every year as she collected new items and disposed of the old fashions. Nonetheless, she felt a growing sense of discontentment in herself and with Chase. While her social media posts continued to portray the #powercouple, they became less frequent as she could hardly stand to post pictures and text that were so foreign to her actual experience. When disagreements arose with Chase, she would quickly find herself crying and criticizing herself: "I don't know why I do this, I just do it."

Displays of inadequacy were common: in spite of her participation in a competitive power-lifting team in college, she complained that suitcases and garbage bags were "too heavy...can you do it for me?" When Chase would storm out in anger, she would feel relieved, until he came back, at which time she would inexplicably dissolve into tears, even though there had been several hours to cool down after the initial blow-up. When she was offered a promotion at work that would offer her twice her current salary (much more than Chase made), she turned it down, explaining that she had "too much going on right now in life, I don't feel like I'm ready for that kind of a step." Upon discovering illicit text messages between Chase and his paramour, Mary resolved to leave him, until it came time to communicate this information to him. Instead, she found herself calling him a liar and adulterer, berating him for close to an hour. When Chase attempted to defend himself, she collapsed into tears, and spent the next hour pointing out all of her flaws: "I guess I'm just not pretty enough, I guess I should wear sexier clothes. I guess I just am bad in bed."[18]

Things had, clearly, gotten quite out of control. They agreed (for the first time in years) to do something important together: go back to therapy. They worked together to find a counselor in town that neither of them knew, and agreed that it didn't matter how much the sessions cost: it was worth it to try to save the marriage.

18 Translation: "Look how horrible you've made me feel about myself! Now, you're going to have to make up for it, whether through reassurance or penitence."

This second counselor, like the first, helped immensely by simply listening and working to understand their feelings and perspectives. Unlike the first, this counselor oriented them both towards a glaringly obvious reality: *they were in competition with one another, and had failed to cooperate for the vast majority of their relationship.*

The counselor helped them understand that they had both, in their own ways, made sense of their childhood experiences by adopting a competitive style of life. Chase, she noticed, was a second-born with an incredibly successful sister two years older than him. She was a gifted dancer, a straight-A student, and a "goody-two-shoes." Chase was openly compared to his sister on numerous occasions growing up, and these comparisons were invariably discouraging to him.

When the counselor asked for his earliest memory of life, Chase reported:

> *I am four years old, and my mom and sister are making bread together. My sister is tall enough to reach everything on the counter, but I'm not. So I'm trying to stand on my tiptoes so I can show her I can do it too. My mom swats my hand, and tells me that I'm too small, and that I need to find something else to do. I don't know what to do, so I go over and get my crayons and paper. I write the word "bread" on the paper, and my mom can't believe it, because I was so little. She said that my sister hadn't learned to write until first grade, and was happy with me.*

The counselor pointed out Chase's fundamental awareness of competition between himself and (notably) a female figure. She also observed his compensation for feeling too small: he demonstrated his intellectual prowess and excellence as a way to defeat his sister.

Chase also shared a recurring dream from childhood:

> *I'm in a bank by myself, but the tellers are there. This huge giant walks in and starts breaking everything on the walls. This person at the bank hands me this big bag of money. It's really heavy but I'm strong enough to hold it. They tell me "Throw it!" I throw the bag at the giant and it hits it in between the eyes, like in David and Goliath. The giant falls down and then I get to keep the money.*

It turns out Chase grew up in a home with not much money, and—as the counselor pointed out— money meant power in Chase's family. It also appears that money was a way to defeat big challenges, which often took the metaphorical shape of "Goliaths" in need of slaying.

Mary also learned about herself. As an only child, Mary spent her childhood watching her parents' relationship. Her father was an incredibly successful businessman, a self-made millionaire. "Father"— as she called him— often touted the importance of hard work, telling her "It's the only way to get ahead in life; otherwise, people will take all the best things in life for themselves and run all over you." Mom was often bossed around and— frankly— bullied by her father. Her mother was heavy, and didn't make much of an effort to look nice, which served as a constant irritation to her husband. He wanted a nice-looking woman on his arm at the high society parties he attended. Mary's mother told her "Don't be like me; you've got to carve out a place in life for yourself, or else you'll end up like me, a sidekick to someone else."

Mary's earliest memory went like this:

> *I'm three, and I'm playing a game with mom. I start to throw around these big puzzle pieces, and they are getting everywhere, but we're having a great time with it and laughing. Then dad comes in, and he gets so mad at mom and starts yelling at her to clean it all up. She starts to do it. Then my dad looks at me and sees me crying, and says "You're lucky you're so cute, I can't be mad at you."*

Mary also had a recurring dream from childhood:

> *There's a mean boy on the playground who won't let me play kickball, so I start to cry. He sees that and he feels so bad, he lets me play then and lets me be the pitcher. Everyone is glad that I'm pitching because I throw it right every time.*

The counselor aptly observed that Mary, too, had been trained to manage life as a competitor. Her life felt like an opportunity to dominate or be dominated. She had from an early age given an understandable— but mistaken— meaning to life: *Life means— win battles through beauty or tears, or else you'll get bullied.*

Upon seeing their lifelong patterns of competition, Mary and Chase were amazed, and deeply saddened. They were exhausted from years of competitive striving against one another. They felt a deep sense of loss over the time they had wasted plotting revenge, struggling for power, and failing to cooperate. But what now? Chase had been unfaithful. Mary, much to her chagrin, had turned into a bit of a brat, getting her way in whatever way possible.

How would they get out of this mess?

The counselor suggested a different life meaning for them to consider: *Life means— be excellent so as to contribute to the well-being of other people*. There was no use in doing away with their drive for excellence. But they could stand to do away with the drive to defeat one another. She suggested that they make a list of five items. This time, no deal-breakers. Rather, they were to make a list of five ways to contribute in a significant way to the other.

It immediately occurred to both Chase and Mary that they had been so busy defeating each other that they hadn't even considered how to be helpful. Even when Chase brought home flowers, he was aware that it was a bargaining chip: a way for him to extract favor, sex, or (if Mary gave neither) pity and moral superiority. Mary recognized that even her social media posts touting Chase's excellence were a way for her to improve her social standing among her friends.

The counselor's assignment was one of many, but over the course of a few months, Chase and Mary were now catching themselves[19] in competition. When they did catch themselves, they were reminded that competition had brought them to the brink of divorce, and reoriented themselves— however imperfectly— towards cooperation.

Soon they found themselves not just helping each other, but *helping others together*. Mary still spent time on social media, but instead of using it to compete, she offered genuine encouragements to others. Chase still ran the family budget (he was good at it!), but stopped using spreadsheets and found a format that helped Mary make sense of the information. Mary, an obviously intelligent woman, engaged willingly in discussions about finances, which further encouraged Chase. They reviewed the budget monthly to make sure that they both felt they were using their money wisely in pursuit of their goals *as a couple*, not as individuals.

They developed goals and values for their marriage. These included *radical honesty, fun, independence, responsibility, and kindness.* These goals had full buy-in from both Chase and Mary, and provided a framework in which all kinds of decisions could be made. When disagreements arose— and they did!— they were able to go back to these goals as

---

19 The most common homework assignment I give to my clients is to "catch themselves." It is incredibly powerful to see yourself acting in an unhealthy pattern. Kurt Adler, Alfred's son, was known for saying that the best thing a therapist can do for their client is to let them know what they are 'up to.' By extension, one of the best things a client can do for their own progress is to let *themselves* know what they are up to. To catch oneself in the act doesn't require judgment or self-shaming, only a sense of "Oh my, there I go again. It makes sense I would do that; it's what I'm used to. But, I don't have to keep doing it! What else could I do in this moment that would be less mistaken?"

Mutual/Cooperative Goal:

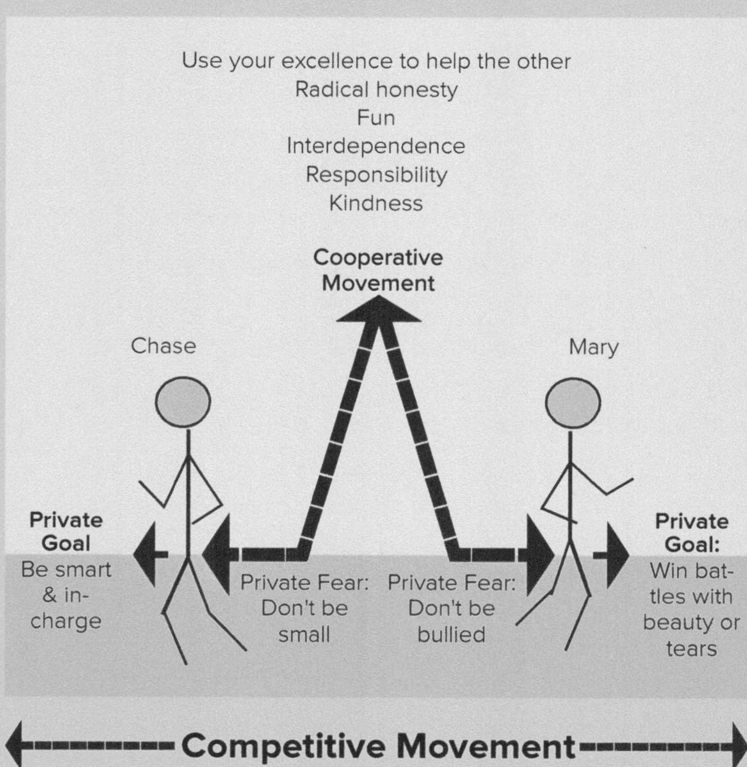

a guiding line, a stable place from which they could always move in *cooperation instead of competition*.

Common Battlegrounds

Chase and Mary's story, while not factually true,[20] is quite common. Competitive, vertical striving accounts for an untold amount of fighting, emotional withdrawal, physical/emotional abuse, sexual dysfunction, infidelity, separation, and divorce. When the goal of a relationship is to gain the high ground and— by extension— to put the other in a "one-down" position, one partner will inevitably feel inferior. When this occurs, this partner will not stand to be in the inferior position in perpetuity. They will compensate in an attempt to gain the upper hand. These compensations will take the form of taking back the preferred position in victory or— if victory doesn't appear possible— revenge.[21] Thus begins the cycle of competition: someone wins, someone loses; the loser compensates and either wins the old battle or a new one, making the other a loser; the new loser compensates....and on and on it goes.

While it would be impossible to detail every potential source of competition in marriage relationships and/or partnerships, there are some common battlegrounds.

1. Money

Whether we like it or not, money often means power within

20 It should be noted that all the anecdotes in this book, while containing elements of true stories, are fictional.
21 Revenge says: "You may have defeated me in Competition A, but I will punish you for it and thereby win Competition B."

relationships. It can serve as a way to stir up all kinds of competition. There are myriad ways to be "better" than someone else in relation to money. Here are some questions that pop up about money within the context of marriages or partnerships:

- *Who makes more?*
- *Who has more "say so" or power over the finances?*
- *Who spends more?*
- *Who saves more?*
- *Who is "better" with money?*
- *Who runs the budget?*
- *Who gets to buy what they want?*
- *Whose permission is needed to spend money?*
- *Who is the "problem spender?"*
- *Who is the miser?*
- *Who is more generous?*

Typical costs:

Couples involved in these competitions will find themselves constantly in conflict about money. Money, rather than being used for the bettering of the family and the community, becomes a weapon and step-ladder to achieve vertical movement over others. It is withheld in order to coerce or punish, and spent to win a power struggle[22] or as way to take revenge.[23] Debt often skyrockets, as fiscal responsibility

22 Translation: "You can't stop me from spending, so guess who is really in charge?"

becomes inconsequential in comparison to the desire to win the competitions at hand. Money is spent on adulterous relationships, alcohol, drugs, and pornography as couples create private financial accounts as a way of ensuring personal victories.[24] Homes go into foreclosure, and a paycheck-to-paycheck lifestyle makes the inevitable emergencies of life catastrophic, rather than just difficult.

2. Sex

Sex is powerful, vulnerable, and intensely personal. When it becomes competitive, huge victories are won and huge defeats are lost. Precisely because of the power of sex, losing sexual competitions is truly terrifying. In competitive sexual dynamics, people put themselves in danger of painful loss and humiliation. It's no surprise that when sex becomes competitive, it's not long before sex— or at least satisfying sex!— disappears altogether. The couple simply decides that it's not worth the risk of losing, and ceases to engage at all. Alternatively, they engage as invulnerable participants, making sex into something only a half-step away from non-relational masturbation. Competitive sex poses questions to couples that spur on contests:

- *Who bears the burden (or right!) to initiate sex?*
- *Who gets to decide how often sex should be had?*

---

23 Translation: "You didn't give me what I wanted, so now I'll make sure you don't have money either, since now we're both in debt."
24 Translation: "You think you're winning, but you don't even know about my secret account over which I have all the control and power."

- *Who gets to determine what is sexy?*
- *Who decides whether the lights stay on or off.*
- *Who gets to be "on top" (literally and metaphorically)?*
- *Who is "better in bed?"*
- *Whose sexual needs are more important?*
- *Who is more sexually experienced?*[25]
- *Who gets to decide what constitutes foreplay?*
- *Who orgasms first and last (or at all)?*
- *Who decides what birth control methods are used?*

Typical costs:

Sex, rather than being a powerful tool for connection, mutual enjoyment, and pleasure, becomes a battleground. Frequency and overall enjoyment of sex plummets as partners tacitly agree to forego the sexual competition in order to avoid the pain of defeat. Coercive and manipulative sexual tactics are used, resulting in serious damage to the relationship. Sexual frigidity, erectile dysfunction, and other physiological issues appear, making physical the metaphysical lack of cooperation. Birth control or— conversely— pregnancy become solo endeavors, creating a deeply isolating dynamic. When competition becomes the predominant style of sexual interaction, couples may begin to look elsewhere for a satisfying sexual experience. Adultery and heavy use of pornography disrupt trust and increase a sense of sexual insufficiency in both members of the relationship.

25 The answer to this question is double-edged. Depending on the couple, experience can mean a position of superiority ("I'm the one who knows what they are doing in bed"), but other times might earn a partner the title of "slut," with feelings of shame/guilt to boot.

Children are— tragically— not immune to the effects of sexual competition, regardless of the level of knowledge of their parents' sex life. They become children from broken homes if/when parents divorce. They discover age-inappropriate pictures and videos on their parents' computer or phone at a young age.[26] Children sense and are affected by the quiet coldness between parents who struggle to engage in even the most basic forms of affection because of the couple's sexual competition. This can, predictably, increase anxiety in children and model problematic styles of interaction.

3. Kids

The magnitude of parents' love for their children is enormous. In my work in parent consultation, I often find that a parent's greatest fear is being a "bad mom/dad." Not surprisingly in parents who are having problems with discipline and behavior management, there also seems to be a strong desire to be a "Superstar Parent." Parents look down on other households, making condescending comments about how others handle their children. Even in these moments of judgment, they betray a fundamentally competitive approach to parenting: "I must be the best parent."

Sadly, this competition is not restricted to the dynamics between different families, but often exists *within*

---

26 E.g., 90% of 18-year-old American males have been exposed to pornography, and the average age of exposure for that group is somewhere between 8-11. Young females are also vulnerable to early and unhelpful exposure.

the marriage or partnership. Competitive partners constantly compete for who is the "Better Parent." Opportunities for winning and losing are almost infinite within the realm of parenting, but the following types of questions frequently spur on the competitive spirit:

- *Who do the kids like more?*
- *Who is the more consistent disciplinarian?*
- *Whose discipline tactics work better?*
- *Who yells at the kids less?*
- *Who can get the kids laughing?*
- *Who attends more of the kids' activities?*
- *Who gets more hugs and "I love you's" from the kids?*
- *Who understands the kids' behavior better?*
- *Who do the kids respect more?*
- *Who do the kids listen to?*
- *Who do the kids open up to?*

Typical costs:

Much will be said of the costs of competitive parenting in the next chapter, which will evaluate the competition between children and adults. However, it's important to not ignore that the competition *between* parents has an incredibly high price-tag. Parents leave behind any semblance of wisdom in their parenting decisions, as what is actually good for the children becomes unimportant in comparison to winning the competition at hand. Some children are spoiled and pampered in attempts to win their favor while others are punished, criticized, and discouraged at every turn as parents seek to show one another that they are the better disciplinarian. "I-told-you-so" conversations are common, as parents try to take credit for their children's successes, rather than encouraging *the child* for positive decision making. When difficulties arise, parents feel alone and unsupported in their attempts to be helpful, as they cannot trust their partner, who is now is their adversary.

Children are not immune to the competition between their parents or caregivers. They feel torn between parents, wanting to avoid hurting either parent by showing deference or favor to the other. This inevitably results in either a 1) good cop-bad cop dynamic in the home, or 2) one in which no affection exists at all between children and parents. Children either pick a "winner" or refuse to do so through emotional withdrawal.

4. Household responsibilities

The daily challenges of life may be menial, but they are not immune to competitive dynamics. Tasks as simple as dish-washing, putting clothes in the hamper, changing HVAC filters, and scrubbing the toilet can carry great meaning. Couples compete for who is "in charge" of how tasks are done, and in what order. They claim positions of superiority by working like a slave, only then to complain about how "nothing gets done unless I do it."[27] They stonewall by leaving dishes undone in order to show the other "You can't

27 Translation: "I'm the capable and hard-working one around here; you're too stupid and lazy to be of any help. Thank goodness I'm around; you'd be a total failure without me."

tell me what to do; plus, you owe me because I did them last time!"[28] Great debts are incurred non-consensually during housework: "I took all the worst chores, you got to wash the windows when it was so nice out."[29] Sometimes work is even un-done and completed "properly" in order to defeat the other in competition. If the bowls in the dishwasher aren't facing south-by-southeast on the top rack, *clearly* everything is wrong.[30] Competition often exists in the answers to these kinds of questions:

- *Who does more around the house?*
- *Who does chores "better"?*
- *Who decides what chores are necessary and when they get done?*
- *Who has to do the most unpleasant things?*
- *Who can outlast the other in enduring a messy house?*
- *Who 'gives in' first and does the necessary work?*
- *Whose chores are more important?*
- *Who gets to evaluate the work of the other?*
- *Who gets final say on how things get done?*

28 Translation: "I won't let myself get exploited, so I will make damn sure that I don't do anything more than I have to."
29 Translation: "I get to keep control of the 'ledger,' and I'll always make it so that you're in my debt."
30 Translation: "You didn't do it my way, so now your effort is worthless. My work, on the other hand, will last."

Typical costs:

When competitive striving characterizes a home, often the home is a mess, as necessary tasks are ignored in lieu of focus on the battle itself. As couples attempt to outlast one another in a kind of staring contest, [31] the home falls into disarray. Chores which could be a real pleasure to complete become drudgery because they represent loss and inferiority. Often, one member of the couple/family becomes burnt out from overwork, as they attempt to prove themselves to be superior in their skill, work ethic, and tenacity. Correspondingly, other members of the couple/family are enabled to be slothful and unskilled in the ways of work. Children never learn to sweep a kitchen floor because mom insists on defeating dad in the contest of "who is more committed to a clean house" before they can lend a hand. Wives are relegated to the kitchen while the husband fixes all the mechanical items in the house, as this is "men's work," which— in his mind— is superior work. Lack of experience and competence is rampant, because there is something to be gained by keeping the opponent inexperienced and incompetent. Thousands of dollars a year are lost paying others to complete complicated tasks that might require dual effort, as the prospect of cooperation is too unpleasant to consider.

The "Four Horsemen" As Competitive Tactics

Dr. John Gottman's work on marriage relationships and life

31 E.g., "I'm not doing those dishes, I don't care if I wait a whole year!"

partnerships is unparalleled in its breadth, rigor, and popularity. As a result of his research, Gottman (1994) identified "Four Horsemen of the Apocalypse" for marriages: characteristics that, if left unaddressed, will inevitably lead to the breakdown of a relationship. Gottman found that by looking for these traits in couples' interactions, he was able to predict with impressive accuracy relational breakdown, separation, and divorce. These "Horsemen" are: *criticism, contempt, defensiveness, and stonewalling.*

Criticism is self-explanatory: it is any form of communication that brings heightened awareness of a perceived problem in another person. Gottman defines the other three "Horsemen" in detail:

"**Contempt**...involves any insult, mockery, or sarcasm or derision of the other person. It includes disapproval, judgment, derision, disdain, exasperation, mockery, put downs, or communicating that the other person is absurd or incompetent" (p. 24).

"**Defensiveness** is some attempt to ward off or protect one's self from perceived attack. There may be a denial of responsibility for the problem, a counter[-]blame, or a whine.... The typical defensive statement is self-protective and avoidant of blame and responsibility. The defender appears to feel picked on unfairly and victimized" (pp. 25-27).

"In **stonewalling**, the listener presents a stone wall to the speaker. He or she does not provide the usual backchannels that tell the speaker that the listener is tracking...Emotionally, stonewalling often is perceived by the speaker as detachment, disapproval, smugness, hostility, negative judgment, disinterest, and coldness" (p 141).

When considered in the light of competition and cooperation, it is clear why these "Four Horsemen" are so destructive: they are competitive tactics that prevent cooperation.

Criticism achieves vertical movement by elevating the self above the other. "You're the problem here, not me." **Contempt** is, according to Dr. Paul Rasmussen, the "distancing emotion." It serves to win a competition by putting another down by virtue of emotional distancing. "You're horrible; can't you see that I'm out of your league? Don't bother trying to compete with me, you're pathetic." **Defensiveness** serves to protect against the inferiority feelings inevitably brought on by competitive striving within a relationship. "You think you're above me, but I'm not the problem here: it's you!" **Stonewalling** is simply a way of quitting or changing the game.[32] "I am not listening to you. There's really no way to defeat me, because I won't even participate in your game."

Tragically, the competitive benefits come with a hefty price tag: lack of cooperation and the absence of its benefits. Criticism and contempt, in their fixation on error and defunct character in the other, increase barriers to cooperation by focusing on division and difference rather than on mutual

32 See Chapter I: "Striving, But For What?"

benefit and challenge, thus cutting off opportunities for togetherness. *Life means— if other people are the problem, you're not.* Each partner is so interested in putting the other down to gain the position of superiority that they forget the shared problem.

Mark points out that Nancy is a nag, and Nancy sarcastically replies "Oh, yes Mark, I'm sure if I left you to your own devices, you'd *totally* remember your sister's birthday gift." The argument goes on and on— poor Mark's sister doesn't get her gift any faster, in large part because Mark and Nancy have refused to cooperate, opting for competitive striving.

Defensiveness inhibits cooperation by making self-protection a higher goal than mutual problem-solving, often at the expense of the other. *Life means— I must never suffer insult or injury from another.* Each partner is so obsessed with avoiding the "slings and arrows" thrown by the other that they forget about the real challenges at hand. Jeremy responds to Emily's complaint about his spending habits by insisting that "I only ever buy things that I need, you'd have me starving and in rags if it were up to you!" Emily protests: "Are you kidding me? I am always thinking about how to give you what you need, and even more. I just don't have any interest in going into debt, like you!" Both Jeremy and Emily forget the real challenge: setting up a family budget together. Jeremy maintains his dignity as a "Justified Spender;" Emily keeps her place of honor as "Responsible Treasurer." Debt still piles up, and no budget ever gets made.

Stonewalling inhibits cooperation through the means

of simple refusal to participate in any kind of cooperative task, even conflict. *Life means— don't play any game you won't win*. Both partners are so intent on not losing a battle that they disengage completely from the necessary components of conflict and disagreement. Luke tries to confront Sylvia in the morning about the out-of-control drinking that resulted in her vomiting for several hours the night before. Sylvia closes her eyes, puts on a blank face, and takes occasional peeks at Luke through barely-open lids that demonstrate her boredom and apathy. When Luke demands to know whether she's "hearing" him, she sighs slowly and nods her head in an almost imperceptible movement. Luke throws up his hands, walks out of the room, and mumbles on his way out. Sylvia's slowly-developing substance abuse problem related to her dissatisfaction with the division of labor at home goes unaddressed. There's no room for cooperation in reordering the marital roles, because conversation has been shut down completely in order to ensure the avoidance of defeat.

The golden thread running through Gottman's Four Horsemen is this: competitive striving determines the behavior, rather than cooperative striving. Criticism, contempt, defensiveness, and stonewalling make no sense within what Adler called the "iron-clad logic of social living" (cooperation), but only within the context of a competitive goal. When seeking the excellence of the relationship is the goal rather than elevating the self above the other, these behaviors and tactics will disappear naturally, not because of *skill development* but rather *goal adjustment*.

Competition & Cooperation in Couples' Therapies

A number of therapeutic approaches present avenues for improved relationships. Some focus on teaching and developing communication skills to improve conflict management, while others use assessments to improve mutual understanding. Psychodynamic approaches deal with past traumas and adverse experiences, and attachment-focused approaches seek to improve feelings of belonging and security. These approaches may seem as though they are addressing a wide variety of concerns. Yet every approach, at its core, is essentially seeking to improve cooperation and reduce competition.

Communication-based strategies emphasize the importance of de-escalation and intentional use of language. E.g., rather than saying "you always forget to lock the door," a wife can improve her communication by saying "I noticed you didn't lock the door; it's upsetting to me when you forget." Rather than a husband insisting "Carla, you *never* stick up for me," he could say "When you laughed at me along with everyone else tonight, I felt very alone." These very meaningful improvements can be rehearsed ad nauseam in therapy sessions, yet sometimes the rehearsals result in no improvement. Why?

Too often therapists and other helping professionals write off this lack of progress as vague, unexplainable "resistance," when in fact it is due to a problem of competition. De-escalation of comments reduces the competitive power of comments. Pointing out to a husband that he forgot to lock the door a few minutes ago puts him down a little bit, but that might not cut it if the wife is compensating for strong feelings of inferiority herself. If, instead, the husband is a person who "always" forgets, the wife has now put him in the category of "stupid," "irresponsible," or "careless." The wife wins the competition *precisely* because she insists on using the word "always," and as long as she seeks to win a competition, it is unlikely that she will make the meaningful change rehearsed in counseling.

If couples remain in competition, even genuinely helpful communication strategies will not be utilized. If, however, the couple can be won over to a cooperative understanding of their relationship— the realization that there is much more to be gained from being unified, respectful, and helpful— these new communication strategies will become useful and catch on quickly.

Assessment-based approaches emphasize the importance of mutual understanding. E.g., if extraverted Miranda can learn about Rick's introversion, she'll be more empathetic and understanding when he's less-than-excited to attend the fifth social gathering this week. But— again— it sometimes happens that in spite of the most powerful and informative assessments, even when interpreted and communicated masterfully by the therapist, the Mirandas of the world persist in their exasperation with the Ricks. Why?

Vague resistance is— predictably— seen as the culprit. Yet, a closer look will reveal that Miranda and Rick treat each other as adversaries.

Miranda understands that Rick is an introvert; but in

her view, his introversion is a competing way of doing life that she must defeat with her "extraverted way." Empathy and thoughtfulness for Rick would inhibit her ability to crush him with her insistence that they "go out." She won't ever agree to attend anything alone: Rick *must* attend, because if he doesn't, he wins! Rick likewise competes, complaining about the outings and always moving slowly to ensure a late arrival. In this way, he defeats her extraversion by passively asserting his introversion. He will go, but won't talk to anyone and makes sure she doesn't have a good time.

If Miranda and Rick could cooperate by understanding that the other's personality is an asset to the relationship, empathy, boundaries, self-reliance, and kindness would take root. Miranda could learn the precious skill of solitude and quality time and Rick could expand his social network and breadth of experience. If they adopt a horizontal, cooperative style of striving, the knowledge they have of each other from the assessments become plowshares (a necessary tool for growth) rather than swords (a necessary tool for destruction).

Psychodynamic approaches emphasize the need to work through past traumas and experiences in order to avoid unconscious processes that cause conflict and hurt. For example, Michaela's rape at the age of 16 has a massive impact on her sex life with Zach; Zach's abuse at the hands of his father has significantly affected his own difficulty managing anger. Why then — if Michaela has processed her rape, and Zach his abuse in individual therapy — do they continue to have infrequent, cold, and emotionally painful sex? Why does Zach continue to blow his lid when in conflict with Michaela?

In no way should the abuse that they suffered be minimized, but in reality, their trauma histories are not their biggest problem in marriage. Rather, it's competition.

Michaela, after being raped, very understandably came to an unconscious decision: "Never again will I be in a position of sexual powerlessness." This decision helped her immensely by keeping her safe, even helping her to fight off an attacker when she was in college. Unfortunately, it also solidified a fundamentally competitive style of sexual behavior. She insists that she be on top during sex, something Zach is "ok with" but doesn't particularly enjoy. She puts immense pressure on Zach to perform what she likes during sex, causing Zach to feel inferior. This has predictable results: Zach loses erections, loses interest, and begins to feel used. In turn, Michaela notices his waning or non-existent interest, and feels inferior herself: "Am I not sexy enough?"[33]

To avoid these feelings of inferiority, Michaela simply forgoes sex, as it is not a competition she feels she can win. Zach, while unsatisfied, isn't particularly drawn to working on the sexual relationship, as he also finds it to be a battleground that usually results in defeat. He feels chronically insufficient and criticized: who would want that?

Zach, after being brutally punished by his father for

---

33 While not always true, physical beauty is often a primary form of sexual power, particularly for females. If a female begins to feel as though she is no longer "sexy," that often corresponds to a loss in sexual power. To someone like Michaela with a traumatic sexual history, such a loss of power can feel unbearable and remind them of traumatic experiences in which they were deprived of power.

minor (and sometimes non-existent) infractions at home, also came to an understandable decision about life: "Never again will I be the weak one getting hurt." Like Michaela, Zach was helped immensely by this decision. At the age of 15, after being pushed up against a wall by his father, he punched his dad in the chest so hard that he cracked a rib. His father never touched Zach again. He became one of the stronger boys at school. Notably, his broad shoulders were part of what Michaela found so attractive about him when they started dating.

The benefits of insisting on a position of strength were tangible, but not free of charge. Zach also adopted a fundamentally competitive style of conflict management: others are opponents and must be overpowered before they hurt you. Michaela, when disagreements arise, is his opponent, not his partner. Zach calls upon his anger[34] in order to overpower her in conflict. Even though he hates how much he sounds like his father, Zach yells his way through countless disagreements.

No matter how much insight Michaela and Zach gain about their past traumas, they will not give up their current behaviors until they cease striving on the vertical plane. Their current strategies are simply too valuable in regard to a

34 People often say "I was overcome by anger" or "My temper got the better of me." The idea that anger is an external force that overtakes or dupes us is patently false. Anger is an emotional state that we call into being with the goal of overpowering others, especially when we perceive others as standing between us and something to which we feel entitled.

competitive goal. Michaela's sexual power is indisputable; Zach's ability to overpower through anger is unrivaled. If instead, Zach and Michaela can adopt a cooperative goal in which they can be of help and support to one another and the marriage itself, their current behaviors become completely unnecessary. Michaela, when willing to cooperate with Zach sexually, will find him highly interested in mutual pleasure and a gentle participant in foreplay and intercourse, making irrelevant her protective and competitive strategies. Zach, when willing to work alongside Michaela to find mutual solutions to challenges, will find her to be a kind and thoughtful helper, rather than a hurtful opponent. His desire to overpower her will fade as he sees her willingness to cooperate. If they are on the same team, there is no advantage in putting her down with his anger.

Experiential/attachment-based approaches seek to create healthy attachment or intervene to heal unhealthy attachment styles. Great emphasis is put on active listening, eye contact, physical touch, personal safety, and mutual respect. Theorists and therapists like John Gottman, John Bowlby, Sue Johnson, and others have exposed the importance of attachment and attachment styles in relationships. Approaches like Emotionally-Focused Therapy (EFT) are evidenced-based and offer meaningful help to many couples. But like any other approach, sometimes what looks like a fool-proof approach to helping couples yields few results. Why? Competitive striving gets in the way of the development of healthy attachments.

Kyle has the sense that if he lets others get too close

to him, they will only hurt and exploit him for their benefit. Linda feels that without a close attachment, she's hopelessly alone and destined to face unmanageable challenges by herself. As you might imagine, when Kyle and Linda get married, things get unpleasant in a hurry.

Linda's incessant attempts to attach and "grab hold" of Kyle are— in his view— desperate attempts to control, exploit, and hurt him. This predictably causes Kyle to withdraw all the more: he spends late nights at the office, shows up late to the few planned dates they have, and pulls away from Linda's physical touch, which he finds to be "too harsh" and "grabby." Kyle's withdrawal predictably creates intense anxiety in Linda. She asks herself "Why doesn't he love me? When is he going to not come home at all, and leave me here by myself to handle everything alone? I can't make it!" Their couples therapist deftly navigates an attachment-focused case conceptualization, yet her recommendations for change are rarely put into practice. Why?

Very subtly, Kyle and Linda are in a vicious competition with one another. Kyle defeats Linda in his game of "Who is least vulnerable?" He maintains an upper hand in the competition by keeping her at arm's length. On top of this, he earns her constant pursuit, which— although annoying at times— affords him the benefit of never having to pursue her.

Linda, on the other hand, competes with Kyle in her own game: "Who is the most loving?" As she equates Kyle's withdrawal to a lack of loving feeling and character, she consistently wins the top spot on the podium. While she's chronically anxious about his withdrawal, she also nurtures a sense of superiority. She even tells herself: "If we ever split up, it'll be because he leaves me; I would never do that."[35] She is able to keep him in a one-down position, given her complaints and criticisms about his lack of initiative.[36]

Therefore, the recommendations from their therapist— all brilliant and effective ways of constructing a healthy attachment— are disruptive to their competitive goals. As long as their goal remains competitive (to keep the "upper hand" in the relationship through self-protection or control of the other), mutual respect and safe engagement strategies with the other will not be used. If, on the other hand, Kyle and Linda can be won over to cooperative goals, they will give up their old ways of doing life and readily accept the recommendations of their therapist to begin building healthy attachment.

Kyle can be persuaded, for instance, that with Linda on his team, he's in a better place to protect himself from *real* dangers of being hurt and exploited by others. If Linda is cooperating with him, what has he to fear beyond occasional mistakes and misunderstandings? Linda, likewise, can be persuaded that if she were to cooperate with Kyle, rather than trying to "capture" him, it is more likely that she'll have a true

---

35 Translation: "There's no way for me to fail or be a 'bad wife,' 'because Kyle has all the power."

36 Of course, Kyle never is given much of a chance to initiate, seeing as how she snatches this privilege away at the earliest possible moment. Her actions are not unlike kids calling "shotgun" to get the front seat in a car ride.

partner and friend with whom she can face life challenges. If he doesn't need to be captured, but rather can be won over with mutual respect, why should she fear his abandonment and act as a desperate captor?

Love as Cooperation

Marriages and life partnerships are, in many ways, archetypal relationships. In the Biblical text, the relationship between Adam and Eve is the moment in which human beings first become aware of their belongingness with one another.[37] In this sense, these relationships are also an archetypal playing field for cooperation or— unfortunately— competition. The power of these relationships are indisputable, but as my Papaw used to tell me, "Power is morally neutral." Powerful things can serve good or serve evil. Dynamite can quickly bore a tunnel through a mountain to improve the safety of travel and trade. It can also be used to blow up people in an act of violence. Marriages and life partnership, like dynamite, offer us some of the most validating experiences available to humankind, but also offer us opportunities for hurt, pain, frustration, loss, and anger that are unparalleled.

Beyond their power to affect the marriage or partnership dyad, couples have power to influence those with whom they have contact. Children, for instance, learn how relationships work (or don't work!) by watching their parents'

37 "This, at last, is bone of my bones and flesh of my flesh!" (Genesis 2:23, English Standard Version).

interactions. Additionally, the couple brings their competitive and cooperative patterns with them into their respective workplaces, communities, and friendships. Inferiority feelings created in marriages or partnerships don't stay within the dyad. They demand compensations in life outside of the relationship.

It is of great consequence whether we learn to cooperate with our spouses and/or life partners. If not, relational satisfaction will plummet, along with our ability to engage in the kinds of interventions that empower us to repair damaged trust and attachments. If we insist on winning competitions against the person closest to us, we undermine our ability to support and encourage the other. Cooperation, on the other hand, empowers us to live in an environment of true and abiding love for one another, which in turn empowers others to do the same.

I would submit that one of the most important questions we can answer in a marriage or a life partnership is this: "Are we striving to compete against one another or cooperate with one another?" The answer will prove to be revealing in diagnosing our greatest relational ills, along with helping explain our greatest relational successes.

Marriages and life partnerships run on love. It is how they start, and it is how they are maintained. But what, exactly, is love? Erotic attraction? A warm feeling in the tummy? Sacrificial, dutiful commitment?

Love is commitment to cooperation with another and simultaneous abandonment of competition with that same person. Whatever your religious persuasion, the words of the apostle Paul in his letter to the Corinthians speak clearly about how love is opposed to competition:

> *"Love is patient and kind; love does not envy or boast; it is not arrogant or rude. It does not insist on its own way; it is not irritable or resentful; it does not rejoice at wrongdoing, but rejoices with the truth. Love bears all things, believes all things, hopes all things, endures all things" (1 Corinthians 13:4-7 English Standard Version).*

- *"Patient and kind": Competition rides on getting and staying ahead; delays caused by another might mean you're losing the battle. Additionally, if someone is "late" or "slow," this puts them in a one-down position. Kindness isn't possible in perpetuity with someone you consider an adversary. Empty charm can be maintained for a time, but not authentic kindness. In pure competition that* ***is not subordinate to the cooperative goal****, kindness is weakness.*
- *"Does not envy or boast": When cooperating, there is no need to obsess over what another has that is good, nor to gloat about having something good that another does not. Goodness and strength are shared within the relationship.*
- *"Is not arrogant or rude": Arrogance is— in essence— bringing attention to one's position of superiority over another. Of what use is arrogance in a cooperative*

relationship? Rudeness is an assertive placement of one person's preference and rights over those of another (e.g., I'll sneeze all over you, because I'd rather not bother with a handkerchief). In cooperation, ***anyone*** *getting sneezed on is no good at all; the well-being of the group (in marriages, the dyad) determines the well-being of the individuals.*

- *"Does not insist on its own way": Competition says "We must have it my way, because my way is better." Cooperation seeks what "way" is best for the couple, and therefore holds individual preferences and styles loosely.*
- *"Is not irritable or resentful": Irritability says "you're on my nerves, go away." This is essentially competitive, because it makes cooperation impossible. If the other must go away for things to go well, then how can the couple cooperate? Resentment holds another in a position of inferiority by reminding them of past faults. Cooperation recognizes that faults have to be worked through together, and that if one member is in an inferior position, this damages the position of the relationship as a whole.*
- *"Does not rejoice at wrongdoing, but rejoices with the truth": Competition loves wrongdoing on the part of another, because it allows us to lord it over them. "I told you so" and "You're the problem here" are competitive phrases we use that reveal the pleasure we take in wrongdoing. Rejoicing in the truth is*

cooperative: cooperation cannot survive on lies, distrust, or delusion.

- *"Bears/believes/hopes/endures all things":* *Competition often leads to quitting, cheating, or changing the game. It refuses to lose, refuses to be put in a position of inferiority. Cooperation is steadfast because it plays the "long game." When things get hard, this enhances cooperation rather than accelerating or accentuating inferiority feelings. Cooperators are able to be charitable to one another, trust one another, and hope the best for one another because they have taken on life* ***together*** *and recognize that life, and relationship, is not a solo-project.*

Conclusion

Competition will ruin everything wonderful about marriage and life partnership, even in the best of times. If couples strive vertically, even the flourishing of a partner will be experienced as a threat rather than a shared joy. On the other hand, cooperation will make even significant challenges sweet. If couples strive horizontally, even the difficulties and struggles of a partner are experienced as a chance to help rather than an annoyance. The power of cooperation in marriage and partnerships is indisputable, and must be taken on as a necessary goal if they are to succeed.

4

Competition & Cooperation in Parenting

Imagine waking up one morning, walking outside your house or apartment to discover that overnight, everyone and everything else in the world has grown four times as large as they were the morning before. Other homes, cars, trees, bugs (ew!), streets, and— most importantly— *other people* are now huge. After the initial feeling of shock and awe, perhaps you'd pinch yourself, hoping to wake up from a strange dream. Perhaps you'd go back over what you'd consumed the night before, ruling out a hangover or dietary influence. It is all quite unsettling, but the discomfort *really* sets in when you realize that things are not going to change back to the way they were.

You feel powerless. Others bustle about at break-neck speed with superior power and strength. You find that while you can speak loudly enough for everyone to hear, no one seems to understand what you're saying. The few who do understand don't seem to care much, as they turn their attention back to what they consider more important tasks: mowing their lawns with gigantic lawn-mowers, typing away on their huge laptops, and texting on their textbook-sized smart phones.

You get into your car, which takes a while, seeing as how you have to stand on tiptoes to pull the door handle. Climbing into the driver's seat feels like something Bear Grylls would do in an episode of "Man vs. Wild." Once you succeed, you discover that your effort was not well-spent, as you can't see over the steering wheel, or for that matter, reach the gas and brake pedals. All you can do is call an Uber to drive you to work. You realize that you will now have to rely on others to get you from point A to point B.

When you arrive at work, it's made immediately clear that you're of no help. When trying to lift a door-sized sheet of paper into the feeder tray on the copier that you can only reach with the help of a step-ladder, coworkers behind you sigh with impatience. Eventually, your cubicle mate Ronnie snatches the paper out of your hand and says "Let me just do it for you. Otherwise, this is going to take forever!" When you try to pipe up during a meeting to offer your opinion on a new business strategy, others blandly look over at you with bored eyes. When you finish, they smile weakly and say "Oh that's very interesting, but we've got this covered, ok?"

Before you can head down to the taco truck for your lunch break, someone straps your waist into your too-big office chair and places a plate of microwaved food in front of you. Fish sticks, to be exact. You *hate* fish sticks. When you say as much, your boss comes over to reprimand you, informing you that if you don't eat those fish sticks, you'll be moved into the cubicle by the bathroom. It smells like piss over there, so you spend the next hour nibbling through those disgusting blobs of fish "meat." Before you can finish the last three bites, your boss comes over, pulls the plate away, and sends you over to the smelly cubicle anyway.

At this point, you've just about had it. You're tired, confused, and scared. You've been bullied all day by enormous and indifferent people. You're now acutely aware of all the things you can't do right, or do at all. At the end of it all, you're *discouraged*: you feel completely unprepared for the substantial challenges of life. You're not sure you belong anywhere, and you feel incredibly insignificant.

This is the perceived world of many— if not most— children. They wake up everyday in a world where most people are bigger, stronger, and more capable than they are. They cannot help but feel inferior as they look around at a big, efficient, skilled world. Along the way, they feel (quite accurately) that they have been bullied by adults who overpower them and wag fingers in their faces. They have been yelled, groaned, and sighed at due to their relative lack of speed and skill in accomplishing tasks. Choices are made for them before they have any opportunity for self-assertion.

In observing this, I do not wish to paint adults as villains. Rather, I wish to generate understanding of the world of children. Relative to adults, they are small, unskilled, and incapable. They haven't learned the lessons that only time can afford them to learn. While feelings of inferiority are unavoidable, when parents adopt a competitive style of interaction with their children, these feelings are only exacerbated. This, in turn, leads to childhood compensations and strivings that are exaggerated. These compensations create almost endless headaches and frustrations for many parents, who feel powerless against the asserted superiority of their children.

What are parents to do? How are they to move away from competition with their children and towards a cooperative style of interaction?

Case Study: Janelle

Janelle was born into an upper-middle class Black family in a quiet neighborhood outside of Dallas, Texas. Her birth occurred without fanfare, as she was the third child born to her parents, Mike and Shanice. The family was well-prepared for her arrival, and she was well taken care of as a baby. She had the doting attention not only of her parents, but also of her eight year-old sister Jada and her six year-old brother Javis. The siblings were affectionate, regularly dressing Janelle up in cute or funny outfits, which earned her smiles and laughs from the whole family. Her health was excellent, and by the time she was nine months old, she had begun walking and even saying some words, well ahead of schedule.

The early years were easy. Shanice was always around to attend to her needs, and because Javis and Jada were both at school during the day, Janelle got lots of one-on-one attention. Mike often came home from his job at the law firm to put her down for naps or catch a few special moments with her while he could. In the evenings, Mike played peek-a-boo, hide-and-seek, and "Papa Bear" with her. To play "Papa Bear," Mike would get on all fours, roar, and slowly chase screaming Janelle from room to room, catching her only to squeeze her with a hug and kiss before pretending to "hibernate," which allowed Janelle to make a brief escape before the chase began again.

Janelle had all the predictable tantrums of a 2-year-old, but was generally well-behaved. She responded to the words "no" from both parents and siblings, appeared cheery most of the time, was able to entertain herself with appropriate tasks, and got along well with Jada and Javis. At church, social functions, and during evenings with a babysitter, Janelle was easy and played well with others.

All of this changed when it came time for Janelle to stop wearing diapers and use the potty. When told to sit on her child-sized potty, Janelle would scream in terror, throw herself on the floor, refuse to listen or respond to Mike and Shanice's urgings, and— inevitably— urinate on or soil herself. Mike and Shanice were understandably confused. What had happened to their sweet little Janelle? Scared, disoriented, and tired of cleaning up messes several times a day, Mike and Shanice tried numerous strategies to potty train Janelle.

First, they put her back in diapers. Rather, they tried to get her to wear pull-up style diapers. Janelle refused, immediately taking them off and pulling on the underwear she had worn only the week before. She often put the underwear on backwards, which made her visibly uncomfortable. Mike, in a moment of frustration told her "You can wear your underwear when you start being a good girl, but you're not being a good girl. You have to wear the diaper!" After yelling this at Janelle, he physically held her down while Shanice pulled off the underwear and put the diaper back on. Before Shanice could put it on, Janelle urinated, leaving Mike's pant leg wet and smelly. Fed up with the situation, Mike thrust Janelle into Shanice's arms and declared "You deal with it!" That evening, mom and dad cried together, frustrated with themselves for being part of such a spectacle, but not knowing what else they should have done.

They consulted books to see what the experts might suggest. Several of the books suggested a sticker chart to reward Janelle for behaving properly. Shanice, ever the creative, made a sticker chart to rival all other sticker charts. There was glitter, there were sequins, there were bright colors. The lines were strait and narrow, making squares for morning, afternoon, and evening for every day of the week. If Janelle used the potty, she would get to put a sticker on the appropriate square. If she got stickers in all three squares for a day, she got to pick a prize out of a "treasure box."

At first, this worked like a charm. Janelle looked in the treasure box with wide eyes, excited about the possibility of new toys. She dutifully sat on the potty until she did her business, and collected five prizes in the first week. Mike and Shanice breathed a sigh of relief, feeling that they had overcome this challenge. Unfortunately, this feeling was short-lived.

After peeing on the potty during the second week, Janelle requested to pull the sticker off the sticker sheet and put it on the chart. Shanice obliged— at least initially. Janelle's young fingers struggled to get the sticker off the sheet, and after a few minutes of watching her struggle with it, Shanice took the sheet away saying "Ok, that's enough, I'll just get it for you." Janelle was clearly unhappy and unsure of herself, but didn't fall apart completely. She then took the sticker from her mom, and moved to put it on the neat, orderly chart.

Predictably (since she couldn't read), Janelle put the sticker in the wrong square. Shanice attempted to correct her the moment before she pressed the sticker onto the poster-board, but Janelle didn't heed her warning. Shanice, who constitutionally disliked any kind of disorder, rebuked Janelle for this misstep, and in the coming days refused to let her pull stickers off the sheet or place them on the chart. Janelle's brief improvement with potty training evaporated; she turned her nose up at the prize box and continued to scream and writhe in response to her parents' commands to use the potty. Stickers on the chart became sparse, then non-existent.

Shanice, in a moment of understandable anger and frustration, let loose on Janelle: "We never had this problem with Jada. We never had this problem with Javis. We just looked them in the eyes, and told them that they needed to use the potty, and *they did*. What is so hard about that for you? I don't know why you can't just do like they did. I wonder sometimes if you just like being bad. You're just being a bad girl, it's that simple." Shanice later felt terrible about the lecture, but didn't necessarily disagree with what she had said. Confusion and further discouragement set in.

Mike and Shanice, out of any other ideas, took the advice of a well-meaning friend who recommended spankings. "You both are too easy on her; she needs to understand that if you don't behave like you're supposed to, you'll get bad things. Just spank her a few times, she'll do like she's supposed to."

Janelle responded immediately to her first spanking. She tearfully (and fearfully) ran to the potty and did her business, but then was eerily quiet and reserved for the next few hours. That evening, when Mike calmly asked her if she was ready to use the potty, she became tearful again as she hurried off to the restroom. Mike and Shanice were relieved that she was finally using the potty; nonetheless, they were unsettled by Janelle's behavior. She seemed more sober and anxious. But how were they to argue with the results? She was now behaving properly.

Potty training was finished, with the exception of a short period of regression soon after Janelle's younger brother Jeremiah ("J.J.") was born when she was four. Accidents began happening every day, but Mike administered spankings when this happened, and quickly the problem dissipated. Janelle obeyed, but also adopted a more hostile attitude towards her parents. They wondered if it was "just a phase." A family friend mentioned to them that four was a tough age for their two boys, too. But they hadn't had similar problems with Jada or Javis. Janelle rolled her eyes, sighed, grunted in frustration, and stomped her way to obedience. Mom and dad didn't know what to do. It seemed they could extract obedience, but they also constantly felt at odds with Janelle.

Her behavior worsened as time went on. She rarely disobeyed a direct command or directive from her parents, but often was found engaging in all sorts of inappropriate behavior. She put J.J. in a closet and closed the door, and then turned up the music in her room to a level at which J.J.'s cries couldn't be heard. When confronted about the behavior, she said "I didn't know I couldn't do that."

She ate all of her vegetables at dinnertime, but made gagging noises while chewing them, one time even vomiting up her green beans onto the dinner table. She was always the last to finish her meal, as she spent most of her time at the table scowling at the less-tasty but more-healthy things on her plate, pushing them around with her fork. Jada and Javis made quite a show of how quickly they ate their food, to which Janelle responded with an outstretched tongue.

Snack food began disappearing from the pantry, and empty wrappers would later be found in a wad underneath her mattress. Next to the wrappers, they also found some of J.J.'s clothes that they had thought were lost in a rare trip to the laundromat when the dryer needed repairs. Why was she stealing? They had repeatedly told her about the importance of respecting other people's things. In response to her deception, Mike and Shanice gave her a spanking and then removed several items from her room: her small Bluetooth speaker that she had gotten for Christmas last year and would often use to listen to music, her handheld gaming device, and a plastic basketball hoop that hung on the back of her door. Janelle cried for several hours, but then came downstairs to apologize. She promised to never steal again if she could have her things back. Her parents agreed, but kept the items for a few days as punishment. Not one week after this incident, things began to disappear again. The missing items were found in the exact same place under her mattress. Why was she doing this? It looked like she wasn't even trying.

When Janelle started school, she refused to get out of the car on her first day. Shanice walked her into the classroom, but Janelle clung to her leg and made it impossible for her to leave. Shanice threatened a spanking outside the classroom, at which point Janelle relinquished her grasp but screamed loudly. Shanice found out later that day that only a few moments after her departure, Janelle had calmed down and behaved quite admirably the rest of the day. This pattern continued for weeks, sometimes escalating to the point where Shanice had to forcibly remove Janelle from the car, kicking and screaming. Shanice began to wonder: "Am I a bad mom?"

Jada and Javis were both model students. Their homework was always completed on time, neatly, and without protest. Both had immaculate hand-writing, and they were voracious readers. Jada was now in middle-school, and had received a blue ribbon at a recent awards ceremony for exemplary behavior and academic performance. The blue ribbon hung on the refrigerator, and Jada got her choice of what to have for dinner. She chose grilled chicken and macaroni and cheese— usually a favorite of Janelle's. However, Janelle complained that the macaroni was "too dry" and said it tasted "weird." She hardly touched the chicken, requesting more and more gravy but never eating the meat itself. Mike eventually became so irritated with her attitude that he sent her to her room so that "the rest of the family can enjoy the meal that you're trying to spoil."

Janelle's first report card in first grade was astonishing. She was struggling in virtually every subject, with the exception of science. Math, reading/writing, and even P.E. grades were very low. Mike and Shanice were entirely unprepared, as Jada and Javis were both straight-A students. Upon further investigation, they discovered that she had not completed the majority of her homework assignments for the quarter. The teacher also revealed that Janelle often refused to work on classroom assignments, instead doodling at the top of her page. Janelle's handwriting was almost illegible, and her grasp of basic math concepts like single-digit addition was seriously lacking.

Mike and Shanice responded initially by offering rewards for improved performance. If Janelle did all her work for the week, she would get to go out to eat with mom and dad and spend an afternoon at the trampoline park with friends. Initially, Janelle appeared excited and motivated, vowing to do better and try harder. However, after only two weeks, Janelle began missing assignments and refusing to do her work at school. When her parents reminded her of the lost opportunity for a fun day, she replied "The trampoline park is stupid. And I mean, going out to eat isn't that special. I get to eat no matter what. You can't starve me."

Mike and Shanice, again out of options, reverted to threats of spankings for every missed assignment. In response, Janelle completed all of her work, but very poorly. When her parents began issuing spankings for *poor performance* on completed assignments, she then refused to do the work at all, worsening her grades even further. She said "Why do the work? I'm going to get a spanking anyways. Let's get this over with."

By this time, friends, teachers, school administrators, and even the children's pastor at their church were urging Mike and Shanice to have Janelle see a psychologist. Potential diagnoses were getting thrown out every other day:

- *"Maybe she has ADHD!"*
- *"It looks to me like maybe there is a learning disability."*
- *"I heard about this disorder on TV the other day, it's called Oppositional Defiant Disorder. I'm not a psychologist, but when they were talking about it, it reminded me of Janelle. Have you had her checked out for that?"*

Eventually, Mike and Shanice gave in and brought Janelle to see a psychiatrist at the local mental health center. Janelle was furious about having to go, and sat in silence with her arms crossed the entire session. Mike and Shanice reported all the behavioral problems in detail, along with chronic "bad attitude," academic difficulties, and low motivation. The psychiatrist clicked off boxes in an assessment form on his computer screen while they talked. No one asked Janelle to share her view. After Mike described her as "mean to the rest of the family," she burst into tears, yelling "I'm not mean, everyone is mean to me!" The psychiatrist scowled and told her to please not interrupt, the "adults are talking now."

The psychiatrist diagnosed her with oppositional defiant disorder, explaining that sometimes "kids get like this, and they just won't listen or mind." He also diagnosed her with ADHD, prescribed her a stimulant medication along with a blood pressure medication to take at night to help her with sleep. (Bedtime was a nightly battle, often involving yelling and multiple trips to "get a drink" from the kitchen, for which she was swiftly rebuked.). Follow-up counseling was recommended, as well as a meeting with the school psychologist to assess for any learning disabilities.

Janelle, meanwhile, was becoming more and more confused with her own behavior. She loved her parents, and knew that they loved her. The same was true about her siblings. And yet, she found herself constantly pulled into feelings of contempt, disgust, and anger towards all of them. Sometimes even the kindness of her siblings seemed to be cause for scorn. Javis, after one particularly nasty fight between Janelle and her parents, came to her room with a smile, and simply sat quietly next to her with his hand on her back. She felt the kindness of his gesture, but it only seemed to intensify her irritation with Javis. "Why does he have to be such a goody-two-shoes? Can't he just leave me alone?" she thought.

Her anger towards Jada was even more intense, especially when Jada seemed to flourish more and more by the day. Jada had become quite beautiful, and regularly received attention from boys at school who seemed to be in awe of her. Janelle found it irresistibly funny when Jada had a roller skating accident right before the homecoming dance, which left her face scraped and her wrist in a cast. Janelle repeatedly called her "Jada Junkface" the week of dance, one time bringing Jada to tears. Janelle outwardly looked thrilled with the result, but inwardly felt guilty. "Why would I say something like that? I'm not a mean person."

Genuinely wanting to change, but not knowing how, she tried the medication. It gave her stomach aches, which the psychiatrist attempted to remedy by changing her prescription. The adjustment helped some, but she often felt "off" at school, somehow more numb than she had been before. After weeks of feeling strange, she determined to stop taking the medicine. She would spit it out while in the shower or into the toilet before leaving for school. She felt a sweet satisfaction when neither her academic performance nor her behavior changed: they were both still deplorable.

Counseling sessions with Janelle were excruciating for her therapist. Janelle often sat with her arms crossed on the couch, offering short and terse answers. Part of her wanted to break down and cry, asking the therapist to please help her understand why she was the way she was. However, whenever her parents sat in on part of her sessions (a common occurrence), the therapist nodded in agreement with whatever they said, and then turned to her with a condescending smile. "Well, we'll have to work on our attitude today, won't we Janelle?" To Janelle, the therapist looked like yet another adult interested in tricking or forcing her into compliance. Little progress was made, and after a missed appointment, the family forgot to reschedule. Unsurprisingly, the therapist was not motivated to reach out, as she also was discouraged and confused about how to help.

In high school, Janelle's behavior only worsened. Now she wasn't just putting up a fight about bedtime. Rather, she was out hours after her curfew, drinking with friends in their mid-twenties. She had picked up a smoking habit, which she flaunted in front of her parents, in spite of the regular confiscation of her cigarettes. She impulsively dyed her hair a bright green, then hated it and proceeded to cut most of it off. New piercings, which Mike and Shanice strictly forbade, seemed to spring up every six months or so. She was dating a boy that her parents had marked as taboo after he was caught sneaking in through her bedroom window at midnight carrying a pack of condoms and a handle of whiskey. Janelle angrily (and accurately) yelled at her parents: "You can't stop me from seeing him!"

Calls home from her school were common. Janelle was making regular visits to the vice principal's office for disrespect towards teachers and staff, unwillingness to comply with rules, and "back-talking." Her parents were confused about how to respond to these complaints from the school. They wanted to help, but nothing they did seemed to have an effect on her behavior. The situation became even more overwhelming when they received a call from the vice principal himself.

He observed that Janelle wasn't fitting in very well at school, pointing out that she could "get a little too *Black*" at times. Mike— understandably— was offended, and asked for clarification. The vice principal replied that her attitude "just seems kind of angry and aggressive," which he associated with Blackness. Shanice, who was listening in on speakerphone felt trapped. If she got angry (who wouldn't be angry?), she'd only confirm this man's assumptions about Black attitudes. If she did nothing, she was allowing this prejudice to continue unabated. She wasn't in fundamental disagreement with the vice principal about the inappropriate nature of Janelle's behavior. How could she respond? Mike and Shanice both made awkward attempts to push back, but after the conversation was over, they felt terribly misunderstood and offended. This parenting challenge was hard enough on its own, but the addition of racial prejudice made it feel impossible.

Janelle was one of three students of color at her school, and often complained of being targeted for her race. Mike and Shanice had raised her to not explain away consequences for poor behavior with racism. Had they misled her? They wanted her to take responsibility for her own actions. Her behavior was inappropriate, and they couldn't— in good conscience— defend it. But how could they abandon her to the injustices of obvious prejudice? This confusion led to increasingly inconsistent responses. Sometimes they "came down hard" on Janelle. Other times they overlooked her wrongdoing out of pity and guilt for not being able to do more.

Mike and Shanice were discouraged, tired, and hurt. They considered sending Janelle away to a residential treatment center or a boarding school for troubled teens. As they began to explore this possibility, they realized that— even given their upper middle-class status— they simply could not afford these options. What now? They had tried everything. She had been too old to spank for years. Rewards were useless, as Janelle seemed to smirk at their offers of improved privilege and comfort. Limits weren't respected. They were misaligned with the school system, and therefore felt cut off from meaningful assistance from administrators. Mike and Shanice were losing their daughter.

A close friend of the family's, only a few years out of high school and quite a rebel in her own right, talked with Janelle one afternoon. Tattooed and pierced herself, she asked Janelle if she was happy with the way things were with the family. Janelle said "No, but honestly at this point, I don't really know how it could be different." That made a lot of sense to the friend, as she had felt the same way about her family a few years before. But, she had gone to see a counselor and things had changed.

Janelle pointed out that she had just "fired" her sixth therapist, and that none of them had been helpful. The friend asked if the whole family had gone. Janelle confirmed that this had not, in fact, occurred. The friend provided her with the number for the therapist and asked her to consider going and seeing him together as a family. "He won't take sides, I guarantee you. He's not like the other therapists you've seen."

Janelle thought about it, and finally broached the topic with her parents. Mike and Shanice were surprised. Janelle had always seemed to hate the idea of counseling. They were desperate for change, so of course they agreed to try one last time. They set-up an appointment for the next week.

Everyone felt anxious in the days leading up to the appointment. Would this be yet another battleground, like the other counseling offices they had sat in?

The day finally arrived. The first five or ten minutes of the session felt familiar: brief overviews of confidentiality, the importance of safety, and payment and cancellation policies. However, the rest of the session was entirely different.

In stark contrast to prior consultations with counselors, the therapist spoke primarily to Janelle. Before asking any questions about her problems, he said "Janelle, I saw on the intake form that you've seen a lot of therapists. I'm wondering if that might mean that you're a little bit— or maybe a lot!— discouraged about therapy. If that's the case, I want you to know right off the bat that I understand that, and that it's my policy that no one is forced to be in here. So, take a quick look at the office door over there. I want you to see that there's no lock on it— if, at any time, you feel that you need to leave, you are welcome to do so and I will not interpret that as misbehavior or disrespect. Does that sound ok to you?" Janelle had no idea how to respond. Most therapist offices had felt like cages or kennels that she had been pushed into. She nodded tentatively.

The therapist continued: "I also want you to know that I'm not in the business of making people talk. You're in control here, so if I ever ask a question that you'd prefer not to answer, you can just let me know and I'll respect your choice." Janelle noticed that Mike and Shanice were squirming a bit in discomfort. She nodded again.

The therapist made one final introductory comment:

"Janelle, the last thing that I want you to know before we get started is this: my goal is not to help you behave like your parents want. My goal is to help you become a person that helps others around her, that cares about whether other people are doing well and works to lend a hand. Does that sound like something you might be interested in?" At this point, Janelle couldn't help but smile, and nodded emphatically now, as if to say *"Now you're speaking my language!"*

Mike and Shanice were terrified, a bit angry, and very uncomfortable. Who was this therapist, and why was he undermining them? Their squirming intensified, and without knowing it, both of them crossed their arms. The therapist then turned his attention to them, and pointed out their body language. "Mike and Shanice, I see that some of what I just said has made you uncomfortable, and I totally understand that. I want to clarify that I mean no disrespect to you as parents. My fundamental assumption about you both is that you have been working really hard to help a young woman (Janelle raised her eyebrows at being referred to anything but a "girl" or "kid") do well in life, and I have nothing but respect and admiration for your efforts." Shanice uncrossed her arms, looking at Mike a bit confused, but feeling more at ease.

The therapist continued: "I want you to know that I have no interest in passing judgment on your parenting thus far, only in helping you have a positive relationship with Janelle moving forward. How does that sound to you both?" At this point, Mike— who had been very worried that this session would turn into a "how-have-you-screwed-up-this-kid" exercise, uncrossed his arms and nodded calmly. This was a new experience for him. He had always felt that previous therapists were *his* advocate in the room, another voice of reason to persuade Janelle to change. He wasn't getting that "vibe" from this therapist.

The session continued, and much was said by everyone in the room, but mostly by Janelle. For the first time in a long time, she felt comfortable saying how she really felt. The therapist really listened, not arguing with her or interrupting her to explain the "rules of life" to her. However, he did redirect her on several occasions: "Janelle, I hear you telling me about what your parents are doing, and that is important to me. But what I'm most curious about is how that feels to *you*, and how you respond to it. Tell me about that. I'm very interested."

He redirected her parents in the same way, shifting *their* focus from Janelle's behavior to their feelings and response. Things became more calm. Several escalations were averted. Importantly, Janelle heard for the first time how scared her parents were about her behavior. Up until now, she had assumed that their only feelings were anger, disappointment, and whatever elation comes along with the words "I told you so."

The hour flew by, and everyone— the therapist included— felt a bit shocked by the impending end of the session. The therapist offered a few thoughts: "It's very clear to me that you three are very much involved in an intense power struggle. Everyone would like to have power, because everyone is terrified of what will happen if they don't. I want you to know right off the bat that I *can* help you with this.

"Here's what I'd like to do. Janelle, I'd like to see you on Tuesday, just the two of us. Mike and Shanice, I'd like to see you on Thursday, just the three of us. How does that sound?" Everyone agreed, intrigued about what would come next.

Janelle's appointment was filled with interesting questions. Rather than asking about her parents, the therapist mostly asked about her siblings: their ages, their genders, their respective roles in the family. The therapist pointed out some interesting dynamics. He noticed that it must have been tricky to grow up with two wonderful older siblings. "That's a lot to live up to!" He also asked what it was like to be the third child of four: "It stinks, really. 'Cause, you're not the oldest so you don't get all the privilege. But you also don't get babied. Like, when I was the youngest, at least I got lots of attention but when J.J. was born, it was like...he was all they cared about. Except when I was in trouble. But I remember when that happened, I just kind of assumed that what I had to do was to be like Jada and Javis. You know, like...be grown up. They made all their decisions for themselves, because they were older and not like the baby."

The therapist seemed to really understand this: "Janelle, it sounds like J.J. being born was pretty tough on you. And that makes sense. Sometimes counselors call it a 'dethronement' for the youngest when a new baby comes along. Because that was so tough, you looked around you to try to figure out how to make up for not being the baby any-more. And maybe— you tell me if I'm wrong— you decided that how to make it work was to make your own decisions, to be 'grown up.' Does that sound right to you?"

Janelle exclaimed "Yes! That's exactly it! And that's why I get so mad at mom and dad— it's like, I can't be the baby, but they won't let me be grown-up either."

The therapist pushed back: "Actually, Janelle, it sounds like they can't really stop you. You've been working pretty hard at showing them that you can make your own decisions. I'm wondering if your anger is something that you call upon to overpower them, to show them that they can't *make* you do anything or keep you from doing anything."

Janelle smiled sheepishly. "Maybe?" *A long pause.* "Ok, not maybe. That's definitely it."

The therapist smiled in return and asked her to share her earliest memory, which went like this:

> *I'm four years old, and Mom has J.J. in her lap. She's feeding him a bottle. I'm trying to show her my dress because I put it on backwards because I thought she would think it was funny. But she isn't paying attention, and she doesn't even look over and she says "Oh that's very nice Janelle" even though she doesn't look. I feel mad and really sad. Then Jada walks in and is smiling and she says "Mom I'm headed over to Sarah's house!" Sarah is our neighbor. My mom looks at her and says "Sounds great, Jada, have a good time!" Jada walks out the front door and is singing as she skips up the street to Sarah's.*

Before the therapist could say anything, Janelle shouted out: "Holy *shit.*[38] It's like...exactly what we were talking about. It was so hard to not have attention because of J.J., but then I looked and saw Jada being independent and it looked so good. I thought I should do it too. That's crazy!"

The therapist ended the session by pointing out to Janelle that perhaps there might be some more ways to make it through life other than being "The Baby" or "The Grown Up" who makes all their decisions independent of limits. "That's no reason to be hard on yourself, though, Janelle—you made sense of the world the best that you could. The good news is that you're now able to figure out if you want to try something else. I think you might, but you'll have to decide that yourself." Janelle left feeling excited, a bit stunned, and even a bit *embarrassed*. Had she fought her parents all these years just because she felt she had to prove that she was a "grown up?" It made sense, but was hard to admit to herself.

38 It is perilous for therapists to have rules about "bad language" in session, particularly for adolescents. A therapist's rebuke for using the word "shit" could be disastrous. While the therapist might prefer more respectful or appropriate language, it is not worth losing an egalitarian dynamic with a client in order to enforce such a rule. I once had a client who used horrendous language during session. It was clear that he was attempting to impress me, and perhaps even frighten me. I did not respond unfavorably, and after three sessions he stopped using all profanity. It is likely that he was testing to see whether he could engage me in power struggle over his language, a battle he was certain to win. Once he discovered there was no battle to be fought, he found his own way to proper language.

Mike and Shanice were perplexed when Janelle had returned from her session giddy, eager to talk about some strange memory about Jada visiting the neighbor. They didn't really understand it, but were thrilled with her newfound enthusiasm for therapy.

At their Thursday session, the therapist began by reminding them of his respect and appreciation for how hard they had been working to help Janelle. He asked some questions about a typical day at their house. Who got Janelle up in the morning? What was breakfast like? What was the after-school routine? What about the end of the day? Who handled chores? All along the way, Mike and Shanice described intense power struggles: repeated appeals to wake up and get ready for school, arguments about homework, picky eating, and disputes about recreation, bedtime, and curfew.

The therapist then asked another question. "Around the age of 11, 12, or 13, we start to make some 'big picture' observations about our family. Sometimes they are positive, and they go something like this: 'My family works such-and-such a way. I love it, and when I have a family of my own, we'll do it this way too.' More often, it's negative. 'My family works in such-and-such a way. I hate it! When I have a family of my own, we'll never do it this way.' Mike and Shanice, when you think back on your family, what is the most memorable observation that you have about how your family worked?"[39]

---

39 "The Most Memorable Observation" is a technique developed by Walton (2011).

Shanice answered first:

> *"I remember that my younger sister was always embarrassing us. She had no respect. We were a really well-known family in the Black community, because my grandfather was a deacon at the church, and it was a small town. So there was kind of a reputation that we had to keep up. All the rest of us were on-board with that. It's not like we didn't want to misbehave, but we just did what we had to do. My sister was always doing whatever she wanted, and making us look bad. My mom did nothing about it, because she spoiled her. My dad wasn't around, he left when I was 7 years old, so he wasn't there to help."*

Mike followed:

> *"In my family, dad was 'on us' all the time. If we did the slightest thing wrong, we had him all over us, telling us how we had screwed up and what we should have done differently. He was a military guy, and he ran the house like that. He was in charge and he wanted everything to go the right way. Like a drill sergeant. All of us felt scared of him, like we were really small. I hated feeling that way all the time."*

The therapist asked for their insights on these observations. Shanice remarked "Mine makes total sense to me. Janelle has always reminded me of my little sister, and I think I have tried so hard not to spoil her like my parents spoiled my sister. Because I didn't want things to end up for Janelle like they did for Missy. Missy dropped out of high school and has been in and out of rehab for years. So for me, I just feel like I have to be hard on Janelle, or else the same thing will happen to her."

Shanice then got very quiet, holding back tears. The therapist waited, and after a few moments she continued. "I also feel this pressure. As a Black woman. It feels like I have to be put together, and that Janelle has to be put together too. It's like there is this image of us that people have. They expect us to be...I don't know? They expect us to be angry and aggressive, and I've been working so hard to make Janelle not be that way. But the more I do, it's not just that I'm failing her, it feels like I've failed at showing that being Black doesn't mean being that way."

Shanice openly cried, finally understanding why she found herself being so hard on Janelle, and identifying the fear that she tried to avoid by taking control over Janelle's decisions and behavior. She also recognized the weight of trying to right racial prejudice through parenting. The therapist observed "Shanice, your hard work in not spoiling Janelle has— without a doubt— helped you and helped her. First off, I want to thank you for not being an indulgent parent, for not leaving Janelle to her own devices. Thank you.

"It's also occurs to me that you're tired. Very tired. You carry so much, not just for Janelle, but even for people of color. Women of color. I can't understand all of that, obviously [the therapist was white]. But to the extent that I'm with you now, I feel some tiny part of it with you, and it is *so heavy*.

"I feel heavy with you, and I also feel encouraged. It seems you've discovered that controlling Janelle is a fool's errand. Not that it's stupid, but simply that it can't be done. She proves that to you daily. Shanice, when we make these promises to ourselves at such a young age, like a promise to never let our children make bad choices, we work so hard to keep those promises even if they're not reasonable. I hope over time, we can help you let this promise go, not because it's a bad promise but because it's unreasonable and unfair to you and to Janelle. Does that make sense, what I'm saying?" Shanice nodded.

Mike jumped in. "Ok, I'm a little confused. Not about what she just said, but about my observation about my family. Why do I act like my dad, even though I hated how he treated us so much? I get so frustrated when I hear myself saying things that he said to us as kids. I hate how hard I am on Janelle, and I don't want to be a domineering dad, but I feel like I can't help it! When she bucks up against what I say, I get so mad and I just try to push her down, just like my dad did to me when I was a kid."

The therapist thought for a moment, and then replied. "I have a guess— would you like to hear it?" Mike nodded. "Here's what I'm wondering: could it be that back then, you felt so small when dad was in power, and you promised yourself 'I'll never be the small one again?' You say that your behavior reminds you of your father's; but, I'm wondering if Janelle's behavior reminds you of your father's behavior too. From what you've told me, she can be critical, loud, disrespectful, and condescending when you're in power struggle.

Is it possible that you keep your promise to yourself by trying to overpower Janelle in conflict?"

Mike stared back in silence, realizing that this was— in fact— the case. Mike had always received affirmation from others about his heavy-hands, as they pointed out that he was "The Parent" and that Janelle was "The Child." Nonetheless, he always felt like he was the small one, not in charge, out of a position of control.

The therapist went on: "Mike, I can't imagine how tough it must have been to grow up feeling so small and inferior to dad. It's also not lost on me that growing up in the time that you did here in Texas as a black man, there were probably lots of other ways that you were given the message that you were 'less than.' It's understandable that you'd want to push against that, to prove that you're strong and capable.

"I bet this promise that you made to yourself has helped you so much. You're a successful man, you've got your own law firm. You stay out of those kinds of relationships in which you are chronically put down. It's probably part of why you married a woman like Shanice, who treats you with respect and dignity. (By the way, thanks for that, Shanice!). I also can't imagine what it's like to have Janelle bringing up all those old memories of feeling small. It makes sense to me that you'd work hard to stay out of that inferior position even now. Who would want to feel like that?"

Mike nodded thoughtfully.

"Mike, it also occurs to me that your experience, rather than putting you in conflict with Janelle, could really help you to understand something about her: she doesn't want to feel like the 'small one' either. And I think, Mike, because I see how much you love Janelle, that you could really help her feel dignified and respected, all the things that you didn't feel in your relationship with your dad. I think we can help you do it."

The therapist then invited everyone— Mike, Shanice, and Janelle— to attend the session the next week. Mike and Shanice, both greatly encouraged and moved, agreed whole-heartedly.

At the next session, the therapist made some initial observations to set the stage: "I think I've got a handle on what's going on and causing so much trouble. But you all must let me know if I'm wrong about this, because I'm not the expert on your lives. This is just a guess.

"I think everyone is in competition with each other for the title of 'The Person In Charge.' And I think I understand why you all might want that. Janelle, I think you feel that if you're not a grown-up, you're not sure you'll belong in any meaningful way to the family. Mike, if you feel that if you're not in charge, you're back in the inferior position where you're not treated like a human being. And Shanice, if you feel that you're not in charge, you fear Janelle will not get the guidance she needs and might end up in a bad spot."

The therapist then checked in with the family to see if everything was making sense, and sounded right to them. "I just want to reiterate, I'm making some guesses about how things might be. What's most important to me is that I'm understanding correctly." The family nodded, truly feeling that this therapist really saw the family dynamic. Crucially, they also felt like *they* saw the family dynamic for the first time.

The therapist continued: "Here's what we need to do. I need to help show you that all competition will give you— even if you win— is a loser in the family who is unhappy and out for revenge. And, on the other hand, I need to show you that cooperating with one another will help everyone. Does that sound ok?" Everyone nodded, looking at each other in the eyes for the first time in a therapy session— *ever*.

Over the next few sessions, the therapist showed Janelle and her parents that all of them had similar long-term goals: for Janelle to thrive, help others, and make her way in the world. He also helped them see that competition for control of each other was no good.

Mike and Shanice were fighting a losing battle. At some point, Janelle would turn 18 or 21 or whatever age indicated her full admission into the world of "adults." At that point, what control would they have? None! The question was not *whether* they could control Janelle in the long-run: The answer was unequivocally "no!" Rather, the question was how to win her cooperation for a short time, during which they could have influence on how she learned to live life.

Janelle, likewise, was fighting a losing battle by seeking her parents' accommodation, approval, and support for whatever she chose to do. She was by no means entitled to her parents "green-lighting" or subsidizing her choices, but often felt that this was the case. Janelle began to see how mistaken this view was, which led to reduced conflict even when parties disagreed.

Both Janelle and her parents were engaging in

battles devoid of mutual respect. Mutual respect says to another person: "I can't make you, and you can't make me. Instead of using force, let's sort out how to solve the problem together."

Janelle, Mike, and Shanice shifted their focus away from how to control each other and toward how to control themselves and their own choices. Mike and Shanice set reasonable boundaries on their participation in Janelle's choices. The keys to the car they owned would be lent to Janelle with the understanding that the car would be returned before curfew. If Janelle chose, of her own free will, to stay out after, she would have to bear the consequences of lost trust and increased hesitancy from her parents to loan her the vehicle. The car keys weren't *taken* (along with a long, loud lecture) as punishment of Janelle's non-compliance; they were *kept* in protection of an asset and her parents' unwillingness to enable potentially unsafe behavior. Mike and Shanice simply didn't offer the keys the next few nights. Logical consequences replaced punishments; encouragements replaced praise. When mistakes were made, Mike and Shanice asked Janelle what *she* would like to do differently next time, always reminding her that there were more chances to make better choices.

Janelle responded astonishingly well. As soon as she shifted her focus away from her parents' choices and toward her own, she realized that she actually *enjoyed* school. Her grades all improved to B-pluses or better. Sometimes she didn't complete homework, but there weren't any arguments about it to follow. School was *her* business, and she could handle the consequences of poor or incomplete work. When there weren't any opportunities to defeat her parents in power struggle by leaving schoolwork uncompleted, she began completing it.

The family made quick progress, though not without difficulty. There were moments when the family slipped into old patterns of competitive striving. Nonetheless, debriefs afterward usually ended in laughter as everyone acknowledged the facts.

> *"Here we go again. I got in that headspace again where I think that it's my job to control you, Janelle. I'm sorry about that. I'm learning, and I'm going to work hard to not do that next time. Here's what I'm going to do instead...."*
>
> *"Dad, I'm really sorry, I think I got that idea again that you should help me and approve of whatever I do. Sometimes I just have a hard time owning my own choices, especially when they aren't good ones. Next time, I'll try to...."*

After a few months of treatment, the family decided together that they didn't need to come anymore to therapy. Janelle was no longer taking any medications, yet her grades were solidly above average. She'd broken up with her "loser boyfriend" (her words, not her parents'), and she arrived at home before curfew most nights. Mike and Shanice felt like they had their daughter back, and were thrilled to see her taking an interest in a local community service project helping struggling middle school students. Janelle's relationships with her siblings even improved, as she began to see them as fellow cooperators rather than people to live up to or defeat in competition.

In spite of her improvement at school, Janelle was— inexplicably— sent to the vice principal's office for "walking too slowly" in the hallway in between classes, even though she had several minutes before her next period. When an administrator called Shanice to report the "misbehavior," they described Janelle as being "lazy" and "too headstrong." Shanice, unburdened by chronic power struggle, was able to advocate for Janelle. "I like that my daughter walks at her own pace, and that she knows what she wants to do. This doesn't sound like a problem to me, and honestly, I'm wondering why my daughter is getting pulled into the office for something like this. Are other students called in for walking too slow?" This respectful confrontation led to an in-depth look at the racial disparities of disciplinary measures taken at the school, which eventually resulted in some policy adjustments and improved awareness.

Years of well-intentioned, skillful therapy (even with the help of powerful medications) was ineffective, not because of therapeutic resistance, but because the competitive dynamics of the family were never attended to. No one— therapists included— took time to understand that for Janelle, the game of family life chronically ended in defeat and inferiority for her *unless* she engaged in unsavory tactics of misbehavior. Even small moments, like having the sticker sheet pulled out of her hand after a successful trip to the potty, reinforced her sense that she was small, she was incapable, she was not "up to par," and she was powerless. Janelle was mistaken, but once she was shown that her family was not on a mission to put her in an inferior position, she was truly eager to respond cooperatively.

The Problem of Reward and Punishment

Much has been written on parenting strategies and methods by counselors, psychologists, philosophers, pastors, and— not to be forgotten— parents! The vast majority of existing material on family health is helpful, important, and insightful. However, the importance of pursuing a cooperative family culture is often ignored.

Understandably, many books focus on helping parents shape children's behavior to the liking and preference of adults. These books end up being some version of "How to Get Your Kid to Stop Doing X and Start Doing Y." The problem behaviors addressed include picky eating, tantrums, disobedience, substance abuse, "back talk," and deceptive behavior. Of course parents want these behaviors to stop. By the time a parent turns to a book for help, they're probably incredibly tired and exhausted. Most problematically, they are desperate.

Solutions suggested in books and by therapists and other helping professionals often consist of a mere behavioral approach: reward good behavior, punish bad behavior. No dessert unless vegetables are eaten. If children do not complete their homework, video game systems will be taken away, and possibly returned to the store from which they were purchased. Disobedience will be met with corporal punishment. Miscreance will be punished with groundings, denied privileges, and— if we parents are honest— angry lectures.

While well-intentioned, the essential problem with these approaches is that they are fundamentally about competitive power. The goal is to help parents "win" the struggle for power with their children. Parents are encouraged to flex their proverbial muscles and open their proverbial wallets. If they want a well-behaved child, they must become more effective bullies or bribers.

When parents employ these tactics, one of two things happens. The first is that children do in fact change their behavior. However, the change in behavior is not accompanied by any change in *character*. While the child will eat their veggies, they will spend 25 minutes pushing them around the plate with a look of disgust. They may even gag while chewing to make clear: "While I'm doing what I'm 'supposed' to, I don't like it, and I'll make sure you don't like it either." The behavior changes, but the environment is just as miserable and contentious as before.

The second is that a child may follow all the rules while their parent or caregiver is watching, but in private all kinds of cruel, undisciplined, and licentious behavior occurs. Children become experts at avoiding punishments and adept at "working the system" to gain extra rewards. They find loopholes in every rule and transaction to maximize benefit and minimize unpleasantness. The child will be kind, but then immediately hold out their hand for the expected reward. Their behavior communicates to others an ethic of "I'll do what's right if and when it pays well enough." Children do this not because they are devils, but because they are much more clever than we care to admit.

The only parents genuinely satisfied with these two results are parents who themselves are infantile in character. Their satisfaction lies only in bending others to their will and preference, not in seeing others— even their own children!— flourish and succeed in their character and willingness to help others. Infantile parents are, thankfully, quite rare. Most parents are genuinely interested in the more important questions of child-rearing: character development, the shaping of motivation, and moral reasoning.

The parents who— for all their efforts and strivings— have only been rewarded with mere compliance, are apt to become more discouraged and flustered by the challenge of children. Most will hang their heads as they make another trip back to the bookstore for another "hip" approach that likely advocates a new strategy but an old principle: bully, bribe, or trick your kids into behaving like you want.

Some parents don't even get to experience the meager benefits of compliance when using reward-and-punishment approaches. Children can react to rewards with ambivalence[40] and punishments with a shoulder shrug.[41] These external displays cover-up an internal reality for the child: Mom and Dad now look like punitive, ill-tempered tyrants eager to lash out, or withholding ogres who want to keep all

40 E.g., "I don't care if I don't get dessert, I won't eat those veggies."
41 E.g., "It doesn't even hurt when you spank me."

good things from them (even the mint chocolate chip in the freezer!).

These perceptions are mistaken and unfair. But children are, generally, not fair in their evaluations. They often overstate their case. They struggle to see good intent behind any action that causes them displeasure.[42] The unfairness of the evaluation in no way diminishes the power that it holds over their response to the environment.

If you lived in a house with a withholding ogre or a punitive witch, you might do what some children do: rebel against your oppressors. It doesn't matter whether the vegetables taste bad or not; they mustn't be eaten, or the ogre will get the impression that she's the boss. It doesn't matter when curfew is; the punitive witch must be put in his place and understand that his potions and evil incantations (punishments) can't have power over your behavior. The actual "game" of life is abandoned in service of power struggle and competition.

When parents frustrated with their child's obstinacy double-down on rewards and punishments, they are missing a simple reality. In the child's mind, better behavior is a surefire way to lose the competition. Parents ask questions like "Why can't you just eat your veggies? We know you love ice cream, and we want to give it to you!" *If* the child's goal is ice cream and a healthy body, then the parents' confusion is

42 Children on playgrounds often accuse another child of "tripping" them when they simply ran into one another during a wild moment of play.

well-grounded. Contrarily, if the child's goal is *winning a competition*, the child's behavior makes perfect sense. The child wins the competition by showing the parents: "You can't make me." Real, meaningful, and lasting change won't result from parental strong-arming or bribes, but only from a change in goal, moving away from competition and towards cooperation.

Rewards Train Compliance and Entitlement, Not Social Adaptation

Alfred Adler (1938) wrote, "It would be a most hazardous venture to expose a child equipped only with trained reflexes or with innate capacities to the tests of a world that is continually raising new problems." The demands of life are constantly adapting, and therefore humans' response to them also must adapt.

Rewards train behavior patterns. Research pioneered by behaviorists like John B. Watson and B. F. Skinner clearly shows that rewards can change behavior. We can train a rat to push a lever for a pellet of food, navigate their way through a maze without error, and accomplish rudimentary tasks using reward. Likewise, we can train a child to put their dishes in the dishwasher, to put their clothes in the hamper, to hang their towel on the bathroom door, and to complete their homework assignments.

What we cannot do is endow a rat or a child with motivation, character, or adherence to principle. In fact, rewards *rely* on existing motivations. For example, most behavioral research on rats that use food as a reward depend on keeping a rat at lower weight than their "free-feeding weight."[43] The reward of a food pellet depends on the rat's hunger, which *cannot be trained.*

When target behaviors cease to result in rewards, they are — generally — extinguished. A rat will cease to push a lever if it learns that it no longer delivers a food pellet. Children, likewise, cease to hang up their towels if there isn't a dollar to collect at the end of the week of towel-hanging — *unless*, of course, the character trait of cleanliness and contentiousness has been effectively developed. What happens to homework completion during the freshman year of college, when mom and dad aren't there to give monetary prizes for academic performance? If a love of learning and work ethic are not developed, the disappearance of the reward will consequently result in the disappearance of the positive behavior.

If all we have to offer children is reward, a question will haunt their mindset and behavior patterns: *"What do I get out of it?"* In a reward-based relationship, positive choices only serve to gain a position of superiority over others by conscripting them into their service through applause, extracting bribes, or adding "goodies" to life. Entitlement and an unwillingness to cooperate with others will grow and become heavily-engrained in their lifestyle.

The question, then, is not how to get *compliance* out

---

43 Free-feeding weight is how much a rat weighs when it is allowed to eat as much food as it wants.

of our children, but rather how to *endow and encourage character.*[44] Character cannot be built by force or bribery, although compliance can be extracted using these strategies.[45] Rather than using manufactured rewards and reinforcements, parents should seek to encourage their children in a more meaningful way: by teaching them the relationship between their behavior and the well-being of the *group* (family, classroom, community, etc.).

Dr. Paul Rasmussen once presented his students with a scenario: a child helps around the house, and then mom offers a big scoop of ice cream to the child in response. He then asked this: what is the *actual reward* to the child? Behaviorists look to the ice cream, along with all the ensuing biochemical pleasure responses that result from its consumption. Rasmussen contended that the *real reward is mom scooping the ice cream.* Why? Because it communicates to the child: "You are important, I like you, I want you around, I love celebrating with you, I feel close to you, you belong...."

True and lasting rewards that go beyond response-shaping into the level of character exist *on the social plane*. What do we mean, when we say "good character" if

---

44 "Punishment is an immediate response to behavior; discipline is a long-term investment in character." Cain, S.; Rector, Village Church, Greenville, SC.
45 It should be noted that while compliance can, over time, become a character trait, this is not a desirable outcome for any child. While parents often take pleasure in child's compliance with *their* directives and ideas, they shrivel at the thought of their child's compliance to "poor influences": rebellious peers, media influence, divergent ideology, etc. Character traits are expressed across situational spectra, so parents should be wary of training children to be compliant people.

not a social character? Good character is a patterned way of relating to others defined by concern, care, and cooperation.[46]

Character Counts!, an organization dedicated to developing positive school environments and healthy skills in children, identifies six "pillars" of character: trustworthiness, respect, responsibility, fairness, caring, and citizenship.

Why be trustworthy? When no one can trust one another, groups disintegrate into factions that compete against one another, finding ways to swindle and manipulate others. Trust is a foundational element of healthy connection between people. If you're not trusted, it's unlikely that you'll gain a sense of belonging with others, at least not for long. If you're not trusted, the people around you will not flourish as a result of your contributions. Think of the Boy Who Cried Wolf: his warning is of no use to the community, *precisely* because he isn't trusted.

Why be respectful? Parents often tell children: "If you want respect, give respect."[47] When respect is absent,

46 Alfred Adler defined mental health as Gemeinschaftsgefühl, often translated into English as "social interest." Lydia Sicher— one of Adler's most talented students— contended that this was a poor translation, and opted to speak of "communal feeling" instead. The idea of Gemeinschaftsgefühl is that we experience ourselves as socially-embedded creatures, that we understand that life is not a solo endeavor, and that the well-being of the community is inextricably tied to our own well-being.

47 Parents fail to recognize the bi-directional truth of this statement. They demand respect from their children, for which they offer the reward of their respect. It hardly occurs to parents that if they desire the child's respect, they should start with an attitude of respect towards their child. There is nothing magical about the age of 18 that entitles a person to respect; rather, people deserve respect *because they are people, not because they are adults!*

relationships crumble and dissipate. When you treat others disrespectfully, they find you to be an adversary to be avoided or defeated. This competitive striving will limit the flourishing of your relationships, and by extension, *you*. Mutual respect is a necessary condition for true cooperation with others.

Why be responsible? If you aren't responsible for your own business, it's unlikely that your business will be properly attended to. Perhaps, for a time, someone else will "cover" for you. Mom will bring to school the book bag that you forgot at home; brother will do your chore for you so as to avoid the unpleasantness of having a grouchy mom and dad. Eventually, they will tire of this and reject you ("I'm not your slave!") or resent you, even if they continue to take care of your business. If people aren't responsible, the demands of the situation[48] are not addressed, and essential tasks are left undone. As long as parents and children engage in power struggle about how the towels are to be folded (and during which 15-minute segment of the day!), the towels remain unfolded, along with all the other tasks that genuinely need to be accomplished in the home. When these tasks are left undone, the group suffers.

48 The demands of the situation are different from the demands of the individual. The demands of academic life are learning and social development. While possibly related, these demands are not the same thing as mom's demand for the subtraction worksheet being completed neatly, in order, and using a pencil, all before 6:45pm. Mom's preferences may be wise, but the distinction between individual demands and the demands of life are essential to developing a respectful way of life that invites the development of individual responsibility.

Why be fair? When there is no sense of justice or fair ness, people begin to make up their own rules or create new, mistaken games. If two siblings are not treated fairly, the child who feels mistreated[49] will rebel against a system in which validating experiences seem impossible. Instead, they will steal, cheat, become vengeful, or withdraw entirely. In all of these outcomes, the family suffers, either from the discomfort of poor behavior or the loss of meaningful contribution from a member of the family.

Why be caring? If everyone looks out only for them-self, it is unlikely that they will be taken care of in a moment of personal weakness or trouble. Caring people invite co-operation and claim social embeddedness for themselves, as others around them begin to see how indispensable they are to the group. Because they care for others, they now have a real and tangible belonging to the group that would be absent without their contributions. In light of their care for others, the rest of the group improves and flourishes, with the result that in a time of individual trouble, the group will be better-equipped to support and help the individual.

Why be a citizen? Citizenship is a sense of belong-ing to the group, an acute awareness that the well-being of the self is inextricably tied to the well-being of the group. A citizen picks up trash on the side of the road because they understand that *as goes the community, so goes their well-being*. No one wants to live in a trash heap. Those who

49 Multiple children in one family can feel that they are the "Mistreated One."

have a strong sense of dedication to their duties as citizens of a family, school, neighborhood, town, or the world become the people that others deem indispensable, important, and appropriately favored.

Character is an assembly of optimal social adaptations that emerge in response to what Alfred Adler called the "iron clad logic of social living," not as a result of behaviorally-trained compliance. The true and lasting rewards for good character are not found in a toy store, ice cream parlor, or bank. Rather, they exist on the social plane in the form of *belongingness with significance.*

Rather than using behavioral rewards to train compliance, parents can allow natural and logical rewards to shape social adaptation. If a child who tends to fight with a sibling goes a full week without fighting, they have already been provided with an immensely powerful reward: improved friendship with their sibling and reduced strife in their environment. If a child does the dishes, they have been able to contribute in a meaningful way to the demands of life for the family, giving them a sense of competence and belonging along with the pleasure of a clean kitchen. If a child picks up their toys, they now get to walk around their room free of the stabbing pain of a plastic block or choo-choo train under their feet, nor do they have to spend oodles of time looking for their favorite toy the next time they want to play with a friend.

Does this mean that every sticker chart or monetary incentive for good behavior is an evil scourge? Of course not. It does mean that, in the long-run, these strategies are ineffective at truly shaping character and promoting social adaptation. When combined with proper attention to questions of belonging and social embeddedness, these strategies can be helpful. If the more important questions are ignored, the best a parent will ever get out of their child is temporary compliance. The worst they will get is an entitled or rebellious child unconcerned with the well-being of others around them.

Punishments Make Enemies and Scaredy-Cats, Not Good People

Rewards are not the only tool used by parents at the recommendation of helping professionals as a way to shape behavior. Punishments are also a go-to strategy. Like rewards, punishments have been shown by behavioral scientists to effectively shape behavior. You can get a rat to do all kinds of things to avoid a small electric shock, and you can get a lethargic teen moving on a Saturday morning by threatening to take their car keys. But punishments— like rewards— cannot endow character, motivation, or adherence to a principle. I've written enough about the importance of character-building and social adaptation in the section above, so rather than beating a dead horse, I will instead enumerate further the perils of punishments.

Punishments are always personal. When children misbehave and are punished, there's always a person behind the punishment. Dad spanks, mom takes the cell-phone, step-dad grounds, step-mom gives a loud lecture...the list is endless. The unavoidable nature of punishment is that it sets one person in a position of superiority, as they claim a position of power over the other's right to a validating experience. The ensuing feelings of inferiority for the punished individual will only invite compensation and competitive striving. Parents who rely heavily on punishment to shape behavior quickly become domineering giants or withholding shrews in the eyes of their children, earning enmity or fearful compliance.

Punishments push misbehavior into the shadows. In a punitive environment, children focus on avoiding punishment instead of working to develop optimal social adaptations. It can be pleasurable to "outfox" a domineering parent, as it serves to re-claim the position of superiority: "They can't punish me for what they don't know, or can't prove!" Rather than making mistakes out in the open where they can be helped, talked about, and properly corrected, children learn to hide their worst deeds and deepest struggles. In turn, this creates deep feelings of shame and anxiety, as the fear of being found out and experiencing the ensuing punishment grows by the day.

Punishments ignore impacts on the group's well-being. Rather than attending to the real impacts of misbehaviors, punishments develop a scatter-shot approach to helping people develop. For example, 6-year-old Billy back-talks and is sent to his room, given a lecture about his "bad attitude." His electronics privileges for the evening are revoked. What has Billy learned? Only this: "Talk that way to mom, and she will get even with you." Billy, who felt superior after talking back, is now put *back* in the inferior position. His smallness and powerlessness prove this to him.

Billy will not stand to stay in this position of inferiority. He'll give an apology (genuine or otherwise) to get back in mom's good graces, or maybe he'll simply make a point to tell mom how awful she is in her revenge.[50] Perhaps Billy will discontinue his back-talk, but undoubtedly, his bad attitude will remain, only this time in the shadows. He'll stew over the perceived injustice of the situation, and he'll become every bit as much of the enemy of his mother as he would have as a "back-talker." He keeps his mouth shut, but repeats all the "smart mouth" comments internally.

Billy hasn't learned the *real* reason to not speak disrespectfully to others. He doesn't know that it hurts mom's feelings to talk like that, nor does he have any appreciation of how to reconcile and take responsibility for his actions. He doesn't know that when he back-talks, he's unpleasant to be around. He doesn't know that mom wants the best for him; in fact, he suspects precisely the opposite. If, instead of taking away his video games, his mother would attend to the needs of the relationship, Billy has an opportunity to learn and grow a more cooperative character. "Billy, when you talk like that to me, it doesn't feel good. Can we start over? If not, we'll just have to discuss this later." Billy's mom orients him towards the real cost of back-talk: a broken relationship. She also sets a reasonable boundary to ensure that she doesn't make herself into a "doormat."

50 E.g., "Jerod's mom would never do this, I wish she was my mom!"

Punishments model bullying tactics that children either employ or fearfully avoid. Parents in my office constantly invoke their "right" to punish as adults and parents. Perhaps they are correct that they possess such a right; perhaps not. Either way, I work to show them the possible implications of teaching "adults can punish because they are adults." It's a dangerous message to pass along to children who will inevitably turn 18 and enter the "adult world!" What will the parent appeal to then? Will they be pleased to see their adult children lording their age and developmental status over younger people? Age equaling power seems like a good idea until a parent learns of their child's bullying behavior on the playground, levied against younger and smaller peers in order to get what they want.

Some children do not adopt the bullying tactics modeled to them by parents and other adults. However, these children often become meek, anxious, and risk-averse as they seek to never displease anyone, parents most of all. They panic when mistakes are made— however understandable they are. They fail to say reasonable and healthy "no's" for fear of retribution from others. They allow their needs to go unmet, take on life as a solo challenge, or become isolative and private. They may find a home with people who approve of their behavior unconditionally: "They're the only ones who are nice to me!" Peers and friends who unconditionally approve of a child's behavior— while perhaps well-intentioned— are the *very* friends we don't want our children to have, as no standard of right or wrong has a place among them. Children don't thrive as bullies or bullied people.

Punishments invite blowback. Individuals will not allow themselves to remain in a position of inferiority. They will, without exception, find a way into a position of superiority. When punishments are used as a primary behavior-shaping tool, children are chronically pushed into a position of inferiority.

> *"You've behaved poorly; now we [those in power] will make your life unpleasant."*
> *"You didn't obey, but we'll have the final word. You're grounded!"*

Punishments come from positions of superiority, and place others in positions of inferiority.

If and when we do this, we inevitably invite *blowback* from children. Blowback is an unintended, adverse consequence of an action. Without exception, children who feel inferior to parents will find a way to get themselves back into a position of superiority by competing with their parents or others.

Some children do this by becoming the "Good Child." This compliance may be comfortable for parents, who sigh in relief at the sight of proper behavior. However, they fail to see that their child has enslaved them. With their behavior, the child communicates: "I'm good. I follow all the rules. Now you owe me your undying pleasure and approval." Do-gooder children often turn into the worst kinds of people-pleasers. They become indignant with and resentful of others who don't shower them with praise. "I followed your rules; now you owe me your applause and protection! Nothing bad should ever happen to me!"

Other children— like our heroine Janelle— gain the position of power through disobedience and vengeance. They prove, time and again, that their parents cannot control them. They become the recalcitrant types who are willing to do anything *as long as no one has told them to do it.* They argue, rebel, insult, and lie to demonstrate their undying message of "You can't make me do anything!"

If Not Rewards or Punishments, Then What?

When parents in my office are able to recognize the dangers and costs of rewards and punishments, they often look back at me with saddened desperation. "Ok, we don't want to reward or punish. But what are we supposed to do now?"

My answer always includes an impassioned recommendation of Rudolf Dreikurs' (1964) *Children: The Challenge*, a seminal work that lays out optimal strategies for shaping character and addressing problem behaviors. Because of the excellence of this work, I won't attempt to re-invent the wheel by repeating all of what Dreikurs teaches.

I then encourage parents to focus on one strategy: rather than competing with your kids for control over their lives, *attempt to win their cooperation in building character.* This sounds complicated, but a few basic principles help it translate simply[51] into everyday situations.

1. Live in mutual respect.

Develop a way of addressing problems that always respects the child's right to make their own decisions, and also respects your right to decide how to respond. If parents focus on what *they* will do, they invite cooperation rather than compliance or more overt competition. E.g., to deal with a picky eater, a parent can set limits on *their own* behavior by saying something to the effect of "Tim, I'm not going to force you to eat what's on your plate. That's your business. But no, I won't go get you chicken nuggets from the burger joint; tuna salad is what you have for lunch."

2. Treat misbehavior as a group problem.

While parents must not excuse a child from the responsibility for their own behavior, they can frame a problem within the context of relationship. This communicates to the child: "We're on your team, kiddo; we're in this together." E.g., if fourteen year-old Libby just told her mom "I hate you, you're such a bitch!," Libby's mother can approach her later on with an appeal, rather than a condemnation. "Hey Libby, I think neither of us really liked what happened earlier. I don't like how our relationship is going. Could we talk about how we can make things go better for both of us?" Of course, it's unacceptable for Libby to speak to her mother so disrespectfully, and her words are not the fault of her mother.

---

51 "Simple" is different from "easy." The act of bench pressing 500 pounds is not particularly complicated. You lift a bar off a rack, let it down to your chest, and push it back up. The simplicity of the task has nothing to do with the relative *ease* of the task. The same is true for wise parenting. Very little of it is rocket-science; much of it is difficult and uncomfortable.

The question is not one of whether her insult was right or wrong, but how to get along so that bigger, *more important rights and wrongs can be attended to*. The word "bitch" is a problem, but a small one in comparison to the problem of a hurtful, adversarial relationship with mom. A cooperative approach helps Libby build character and avoids blowback.

3. Ask your children what they think could help the problem.

When parents determine the "way out" of a problem unilaterally, they are likely to put their children in a position of inferiority by giving the message: "I know what will fix this; *you don't*." Children feel unimportant and uninvolved with the solution if they are not invited to participate in the improvement. When parents *do* invite participation, children feel important and invested in solutions. This invitation short-circuits the drive to compete with parents for power, because power isn't the goal: finding a solution is.

Children often come up with suggestions that are much more effective than what parents have to offer. E.g., after 14-year-old Charlie had a big fight with his younger brother Steven, his parents asked him what he would like to do about the temporary loss of Steven's brotherly friendship. Both parents would have suggested a heartfelt apology and a handshake; Charlie, however, suggested that he cook waffles for dinner: Steven's favorite! While serving a hot waffle to Steven, Charlie looked at his younger brother and said "Hey man, I'm sorry about earlier. I care about you, and wanted to do something special to show you that. I hope we can do better tomorrow."

Not every child will come up with a solution like Charlie's. Nonetheless, Charlie's parents asking for his input invited cooperation and encouraged Charlie to take responsibility for his own relationship with Steven. If they had demanded an apology, it's unlikely that true reconciliation would have occurred. Charlie would have offered an insincere "I'm sorry" in cheap compliance with his parents' demands, or perhaps would have refused: "He should be the one apologizing!"

4. Apologize without tag-along "buts."

Parents struggle to apologize, feeling that the words "I'm sorry" means kowtowing to their child. In this, parents are sorely mistaken. Apologies communicate the humility and personal responsibility that are necessary ingredients of a cooperative relationship. When parents apologize for their misdoings, they avoid putting themselves in a position of superiority that can invite blowback from their child. If children are the only ones to ever apologize, this implies that the only place they belong is in the one-down position. When parents apologize, they model equality with their children.[52]

E.g., after yelling at disobedient Michael and calling him a "brat," Peter approached his son with an apology: "Hey bud,

---

52 For parents concerned that "equality" means that children are afforded all the rights and privileges of adults, a quote from Rudolf Dreikurs (1964) may help: "Equality doesn't mean uniformity! Equality means that people, despite all their individual differences and abilities, have equal claims to dignity and respect" (p. 8).

I'm really sorry about earlier. No matter what you do, it's not ok for me to talk that way to you. I'm going to work on it and try to learn to be more kind."

It is *absolutely essential* that apologies not be followed up with "buts." "Buts" are inherently competitive. They communicate: "I did something bad. *But* you're still in the inferior position. What you did is worse, and explains away my behavior." Apologies without "buts" often invite non-coerced apologies from children, because they can see that the parent isn't seeking to defeat them in competition, but rather cooperate.

5. Use Encouragement, Not Praise.

The distinction between encouragement and praise is not semantic. Pastors, counselors, radio personalities, educators, and physicians extol the power and necessity of praise. This is fair and well-intended, and praise can have a positive impact on some relationships. That being said, there is a *very* meaningful difference between praise and encouragement. One is competitive, the other is cooperative.

Praise comes down from a superior position to an inferior: "You got an A on that test! You did it like I knew was best. Bravo!" The evaluation of the praise-giver sits at the center of what is communicated. Encouragement, however, puts the focus elsewhere. "You got an A on that test. You must have worked really hard on that. How does it feel to make that kind of a grade after your effort?" The focus is on the *process, not the product.*

The advantage to this approach is that encouragement can be given even when things go poorly. If the child brings

ENCOURAGEMENTS VS. PRAISE

ENCOURAGEMENTS	PRAISE
Notices all efforts	Notices only results
Finds the excellence in error	Finds the error in excellence
Focuses on well-being of the child	Focuses on the praise-giver
Remains aware of the learning process	Forgets the learning process
Affirms rights of choice/ consequence	Denies rights of choice/ consequences
Understands before correcting	Corrects before understanding
Invites risk-taking	Discourages risk-taking
Stimulates internal reward systems	Builds external rewards systems
Fosters independence	Fosters dependence on "applause"
Never 'bails out"	Enables and coddles
Can be used at any time	Mostly applied only when things go well

home a C-minus instead of an A, what praise can be given? If praise *is* given, it may communicate to the child that C-minuses are pleasing to the parent, and that there's not much reason to strive for more. Most parents wouldn't praise a child for a C-minus for this reason.

An encouraging parent, however, has plenty to offer. "Well then, it looks like there was plenty you got right on this test. It seems like you're figuring out how to learn what's being taught in class, and you'll keep at it, I'm sure. How do you feel about the grade?" There's no whiff of a "participation trophy" or cheap focus on the positive that leads to complacency. Rather, encouragement sees the process of learning as the most relevant variable, and observes the child's capacity to improve.

6. Take on tasks together.

Much has been said about the importance of children doing chores. Research and observation show that having chores and household responsibilities leads to positive outcomes for children as they develop. However, not all chores are "created equal." Chores can be competitive in nature: "You need to do what I say. Be my servant and take on this tasks that I find unsavory." This kind of chore assignment leads to competition.

However, chores can also be cooperative in nature: "There's a lot to do at home today to help us all have a nice place to live. If we take it on together, we can handle this challenge!" Rather than demanding that certain tasks be done, parents can win the cooperation of the child and work

ENCOURAGEMENTS VS. PRAISE

ENCOURAGEMENTS	PRAISE
Wow, you must have studied hard for that test!	You got an A - you're so smart, it must have been easy.
You played so hard, and it's great to see it pay off for you.	Good job, you won! You are a great player.
Thank you for helping out - it means a lot to everyone.	Good girl, you're mama's little helper.
You got right back up after falling down - that's hard, and you did it anyway.	Oh gosh, I'm glad you're ok! You could have gotten hurt! Daddy's here to fix it.
You stopped that fight with Billy - how does it feel?	You did what I said to do about Billy - good boy!
I appreciate how much the team matters to you.	You're the best on the team, they are lucky to have you.
It must have been wonderful for your friends when you stuck up for them.	I wish other kids would act like you do with your friends - they are so mean!
That didn't work out, did it? I bet we can try again tomorrow.	Oh gosh, what a mess! Just let me do it for you, I guess.
I know it's hard for you; let's work together on a solution.	If you would just act differently we wouldn't have a problem!
Hmm, that looked like it hurt. Maybe we can think of another way to do it that might work out better!	See, that's what happens when you disobey mommy. I don't feel sorry for you at all.

on tasks together. If 8-year-old Sandra's bedroom looks like the aftermath of an F-5 tornado, and a mice infestation has recently been discovered, her mother can approach her right before bedtime: "Sandra, I've got my own feelings about your room; how do you feel about your room?" Sandra admits "It's kind of gross, I know." Mom smiles at her, kneels down, and says "It's got to be hard for you to spend your nights in there, I hear you. How about you and I sit down tomorrow and make a plan together about what to do about it? I'll be as helpful as I can!"

This, of course, may not be the end of frustration for Sandra or mom; but, it has set a cooperative tone for how challenges can be managed, rather than striving for the position of power and control. Sandra also feels important and included in a task that will rid the upstairs of a mice infestation.

Conclusion

Parent-child relationships are naturally prone to competitive dynamics. However, they are not doomed. Basic principles, like those outlined above, can be implemented consistently to strive "horizontally" in such a way that the whole family benefits. Where competitive dynamics rule the day, power struggle or compliance devoid of character development are the likely outcomes. Where cooperative dynamics rule, children learn to attend to the demands of social adaptation, setting them up for a life in which they get along with others and contribute to the well-being of their communities.

Like marriages and life partnerships, the most important question parents can ask themselves about their relationship with their children is this: *Am I willing to forgo competition with my child and instead cooperate with them*? The answer to this question will likely predict a large variety of outcomes, not just in the early and adolescent years, but also for a lifetime.

5

Competition & Cooperation in Sibling Relationships

Most commonly, when parents, pastors, counselors, or educators attempt to understand the behavior of children, they look to the dynamics between child and parent. As evidenced by the previous chapter, this approach is not without merit. Myriad psychological and sociological research has demonstrated the significant impact of parent-child relationships on early development. Sub-optimal parenting strategies result in emotional and behavioral difficulties, while cooperative parenting strategies can lead to positive outcomes galore.

However, sibling relationships are too often neglected when examining character and behavior. Siblings— if we have them— are our first peers, and therefore the prototypical "even matches" with whom we can compete and cooperate. Children do engage in competitive or cooperative striving with parents, but especially early in life, parents seem like a whole other species. Therefore, parent-child interactions fail to adequately train children how to get along with peers.

The goal of childhood is to make childishness[53] progressively useless so that by the time we reach chronological adulthood, we are able to participate in the adult world successfully. To be successful and contributing adults, we must understand how to cooperate with adult peers. Sibling relationships are a vital part of how we form— or fail to form— our ability and willingness to cooperate. Like in life partnerships and in parent-child dynamics, if we fail to cooperate with our siblings due to superordinate status of competitive goals, we create all kinds of trouble: for ourselves, for our families, and for our communities.

Case Study: Jimmy

Three year-old Jimmy was an absolute joy. With an unwavering grin on his face, Jimmy followed the directives given to him by his parents. He went to bed on time, finished his vegetables at dinner, and said "Yes ma'am" and "No sir" instead of "Yeah" and "Nah." He played independently, behaved himself admirably for babysitters when his parents were on dates together, and cleaned up after himself while playing or eating.

53 "Childishness" is not the same as "childlikeness." The former indicates a lack of maturity; the second implies a wonder, joy, and playfulness that can— and should be— maintained throughout adulthood. It should also be mentioned that the process of making childishness useless is a long one. Two-year-olds should not be rebuked for behaving like two-year-olds; rather, they can be redirected and encouraged to grow into three-year-olds. The 17-year-old challenges can wait until they are 17.

When his parents informed him that he would soon be a big brother, Jimmy shared his excitement with everyone. He asked question after question about pregnancy and the baby's development:

> *"How big is the baby today?"*
> *"What does the baby eat while it's in there?"*
> *"Is the baby coming yet?"*
> *"Does the baby like movies?"*

Jimmy's parents were thrilled with his enthusiasm, feeling it to be a harbinger of good.

When his mother began laboring a few months later, Jimmy went to stay with his aunt and two cousins who lived across the street. His mother started hemorrhaging in her third hour of labor, and an emergency C-section was performed. Jimmy's new sister Nora experienced some oxygen deprivation during labor, scored poorly on an assessment performed by the NICU[54] team, and was placed under observation. Jimmy's mother's condition improved after the C-section, but she was also placed on hospital bed rest while they replenished fluids and allowed her to recover from the surgery and hemorrhage.

Meanwhile, Jimmy was getting restless at his aunt's house. After two whole days without contact from his parents, he began acting out. He refused to eat broccoli: "That's not

---

54 Neonatal Intensive Care Unit

how mama makes it, this is gross!" He became tearful and fussy when bedtime rolled around, and was even blatantly disrespectful to his aunt: "You can't tell me what to do, you're not my dad!" She, being a kind and understanding woman, recognized that Jimmy simply missed his parents and wanted to see them. She immediately made arrangements for him to visit his parents the next morning.

Upon arriving at the hospital, Jimmy ran to his father and quickly became his "old self," happily sharing the positive experiences from the two days prior. Jimmy was most eager to see his baby sister Nora. When they arrived in the NICU, Jimmy asked to hold her. His father explained that no, he couldn't hold Nora right now, she had to stay where she was to get better. Jimmy was visibly saddened, but complied and went to see his mother.

When they arrived at his mother's room, he tried to climb up into her lap like he did at home, but was stopped by his father who explained that "Mom has a little boo boo right below her belly, and you can't climb on her right now." His mom seemed sleepy and completely disinterested in Jimmy. She kept asking questions about Nora. When the nurses came in to check on mom, they didn't even acknowledge Jimmy's presence. To Jimmy, this was incredibly strange. He was usually the "Main Attraction" in every room he was in!

In fact, everything seemed strange. Dad and mom were distracted. No one wanted to play. The conversation— rather than being about Jimmy and his interests— now seemed to involve all kinds of adult topics like discharge dates, vital signs, and something called an "APGAR score."

Whenever Jimmy asked his father to explain, he just said "Jimmy, it's complicated, I can't explain right now. It's just how we know how Nora is doing."

Jimmy's confusion grew and grew, as did the frequency of everyone's use of his sister's name. He thought to himself "Nora, Nora, Nora! Is that all they care about? She can't even do anything that I can do." He was beyond relieved when his father informed him that everyone could go home, but annoyed when his father added "Because Nora is ready now!"

Nonetheless, he had a newfound sense of confidence that everything would return to normal once they got home.

This confidence was misguided. Upon returning home, Nora was the ever-present focus of everyone's attention. His parents were constantly changing diapers, swaddling, rocking, singing, and fussing over Nora. Trips to the park were cut short or avoided all together because of Nora's need for seemingly endless naps at all times of the day.

Jimmy could hardly believe it. In the course of three days, he had been demoted from "Main Attraction" to "Mild Nuisance." At first, he was angry with his parents. How could they have forgotten him? Why were they being so neglectful? But little by little, Jimmy realized that it wasn't his parents' fault at all: it was *Nora's*. *She* was the one soaking up all their attention! Jimmy determined that he would not be beaten by this little sister. He wasn't going to give up without a fight.

Jimmy's earliest triumph against his sister came in the form of a jump rope. When he was only a year old, his youngest uncle gave him a jump rope. His father laughed and observed: "He can barely walk, Steve! What's he supposed to do with a jump rope?" Uncle Steve responded "He'll grow into it!"

At the ripe old age of three, Jimmy was desperate to prove he was extraordinary. So, naturally, he picked out the one toy in his box that everyone had labeled the "you're-not-ready-to-use-that-yet" toy.

He spent most of the morning in his room, practicing swinging the rope over his head, jumping just in time to allow it to sneak underneath the bottoms of his bare toes. Repeatedly, the tips of his toes were slapped by the rubberized cord, which was extremely painful. He wanted to run to his mom for comfort. "But she'll be too busy with Nora. Plus, I'm not going to cry about everything like she does. I'm going to be a big boy and keep going."

After a few hours of practice, Jimmy could jump his rope four or five times in a row before snagging it on his feet. He proudly marched out of his bedroom into the living room, where his parents were— predictably— fawning over Nora, who slept on mom's chest, mouth agape and drooling. Dad had his phone out, snapping photo after photo, taking time to show them to mom after they were taken.

Without a word, Jimmy walked to the middle of the living room and began jumping rope. At first, mom and dad didn't look up, but the repetitive sound of the rope hitting the floor was novel enough to pull their eyes away from Nora. Dad's face lit up when he saw Jimmy's new trick: "Look at this! Look at our big boy!" Mom now turned her full attention to Jimmy and gasped with pleasure: "Look at him go! When did you learn to do that, Jimmy?" Dad lifted up the phone and started taking a video, urging Jimmy to "do it again!" Even after Nora woke up from the loud slapping of cord against hardwood, he kept his parents full and undivided attention for almost a half hour.

He had *won*— even if just for a moment. For the first time since her birth, Nora had faded into the background, and he had reclaimed his rightful place as "Main Attraction."

Just a few years later, Jimmy's competition with Nora had only intensified. The first few years of school had been difficult. Jimmy was hyper-aware that Nora had all day with mom while he was away. However, Jimmy soon discovered that he was a precocious thinker, and excelled easily in school. He brought home perfect scores on his spelling tests and math quizzes. He demanded that they be hung on the fridge, above any pictures of Nora: "I'm taller than she is, so my stuff should be taller too."[55]

Nora was now walking and running, and Jimmy challenged her to races everyday, which he won easily. After

55 Siblings often make contests out of the most meaningless situations, like how high on the refrigerator their schoolwork is placed. Children's creativity— precious as it is— also has the capacity to flesh itself out in competitive striving. A child once remarked to me in a session that she was happy that her sister "only got the orange socks for her birthday, and I got the blue ones." Little did this child know that her sister (also a client of mine) had shared with me how glad she was that she got the orange socks, rather than the blue. Both felt that they were victors of the same competition.

each "race," Jimmy would ask his mom "Mom, who won? Did I win?" He would quiz Nora about spelling: "How do you spell 'cat' Nora?" Predictably, she had no answer; Jimmy would then say, "You don't know how to spell but I do."

Jimmy struggled to share with Nora. When she would pull a toy out of his toy box, he would become apoplectic with jealousy: "That's *my* toy, I didn't say you could play with it!" He would often yank the toy out of her hands, one time leading to a cut on her thumb that required a bandage.

While Jimmy was in many respects a wonderful boy,[56] his parents were exhausted by Jimmy. He seemed to demand their attention all the time and had become quite a show-off. They were embarrassed by his tendency to parade himself in front of others, show off a new ability, and insist on the full and undivided attention of all who watched until he had performed it perfectly.

Reports from school teachers noted that Jimmy often spoke out of turn in order to "one-up" other students. He was sent to the principal's office for making fun of a student who had failed a spelling test, and was later rebuked by a teacher on the playground for pointing out how another student in class— who had a mild case of cerebral palsy— was slow and clumsy.

---

56 The term "a wonderful child" too often is a moniker for "compliant." Jimmy was a "wonderful boy" in the sense that he followed rules, performed well in school, stayed out of trouble, etc. Jimmy's behavior might have been splendid, but his intentions were sordid.

When his parents discussed these reports with Jimmy, he excused himself by saying "It's not my fault they can't do it as good as me." Dad, an English professor at the local college, pointed out: "It's as 'well' as me, Jimmy."[57]

Jimmy's competitive striving against Nora, his first "peer," had now been extended to his schoolmates. Having the attention of others was his victory, which he secured by demonstrating his excellence in all things. If and when he struggled at school, he became a tattle tale, insulted others, and challenged the least-capable students in the class to meaningless contests of skill. Much of this behavior was treated with little more than an eye-roll, as Jimmy was "a good kid" and "just a little too competitive for his own good, but he'll make a great athlete!"

Things worsened when Jimmy entered third grade, and Nora began kindergarten. Nora quickly endeared herself to the entire school staff, as she herself had turned into an *unbelievably* cute child. While quiet and small, Nora was tender and winsome. Word spread like wildfire in the school building about this fairy-like youngster, and soon Jimmy's teacher asked him daily "How is your cute little sister doing?"

Jimmy began struggling with his academics. Math, which had always been easy, started to confuse and frustrate him. He even started failing spelling tests and forgetting to work on big projects until the night before they were due.

---

57 Unfortunately for all involved, Jimmy's competitive mindset was not corrected in the same way that Dad confronted his poor grammar.

Grades dropped, as did Jimmy's interest and investment in his studies.

Middle school wasn't any better. Jimmy hit puberty early and started getting large pimples on his face, which had slimmed down substantially over the past few years, robbing him of the "cute little boy" look others so enjoyed. Girls who had always blushed when he showed off in front of them now began to roll their eyes and grunt in displeasure. Jimmy's compensations for these insults (e.g., doubling down on immature flirtations) were all the more annoying and repellent to those around him.

When Nora brought home excellent marks on her schoolwork, Jimmy undermined them: "It's not as good as what I did when I had Ms. Smith for third grade. It's not fair, her work is so much easier than when I had to do it!"

In spite of everyone's efforts, Jimmy's grades, behavior, and overall likability worsened by the week. The one bright spot was his athletic career, although he had such intense conflict with his teammates on his basketball team that he quit and opted for tennis— an individual sport. Jimmy liked beating the kids on the opposing teams, but was most proud that he was better than *his own* teammates. He sometimes attempted to coach them during their matches. "Square up your shoulders! Don't settle for the forehand!" He complained viciously to his parents when they lost matches: "We'd win regionals if the rest of the guys would try as hard as I do."

Things came to a head in the middle of Jimmy's eighth grade year. During a tennis match, Jimmy tore a ligament in his knee, which put him out for the season. A few weeks later, after a tough day at school, he was being particularly nasty to Nora. He pulled her pig tails, and called her new crush Steven a "little shit" while following her up the stairs. Nora turned and faced him, and uncharacteristically returned fire: "At least he's not a failure like you, Jimmy. You act like you're the best at everything, but mom and dad don't even like you anymore, because you're not good at anything."

Jimmy couldn't respond. He wanted to reply with a witty insult, but couldn't think of one. All he could think about was what Nora had said. If he was honest, he didn't disagree. It was clear that he was no longer important. Mom and dad rarely asked him about anything except tennis, the *one thing he was good at*, and now that had been taken away from him. Nora, on the other hand, was thriving in every way. Well-liked by adults and peers alike, she was surrounded by friendly relationships in which she was given ample attention and praise. Jimmy, with the exception of his performance on the tennis court, couldn't get more than a thumbs up or half-hearted "Oh, cool buddy" from anyone. He had fought hard in his competition against Nora, but *he had lost.*[58]

Jimmy's grades worsened in high school, as did his behavior. Trips to the vice principal's office became a regular occurrence, and the reasons for the visits became more serious. Rather than being reproached for an unkind comment to

58 Jimmy will not settle for being the loser. As mentioned in Chapter I, Jimmy — when faced with his undeniable loss— will either quit, cheat, or change the game.

a peer, Jimmy was suspended for smoking cigarettes in the teachers' lounge. "Did you really not think you'd get caught, Jimmy?" Jimmy had no answer, taking his suspension with cold indifference.

He never returned to the tennis team, even after his knee had healed completely. He became disinterested in almost anything other than violent video games,[59] smoking cigarettes, and using foul language with his 19- and 20-year-old "best friends," Patton and Oliver.[60] When he showed up for family dinners (a rare occurrence), Jimmy was eager to pick fights, starting arguments with everyone, Nora most of all.

In fact, Nora was nearly *always* the target of unkind comments from Jimmy. She had developed an interest in ballet and jazz dance, and was doing quite well at it. Jimmy joked that "dance girls are always sluts," mocking her plies and poses by flitting around the living room in front of her. He often distorted these movements to make them sexually inappropriate, which garnered harsh rebuke from his parents.

---

59 Much has been unfairly spoken about the impacts of violent video games on those that play them. It is now indisputable, thanks to well-designed research, that violent video games do *not* cause people to be more violent. However, it would be folly to ignore the psychological significance of individuals' predilection for violent games. In Jimmy's case, it should be observed that in every other arena of life, he loses. He is athletically incapacitated and outdone at every turn by his lovely sister. For someone like Jimmy, the chance to play the role of a hyper-athletic hero who defeats hundreds of enemies every hour is enticing.

60 One contest Jimmy will never lose to Nora is the contest of age. Individuals can accentuate their maturity by spending time with people older than themselves, gaining a few years by association.

Nora, collapsing into tears, felt even more insulted when Jimmy added: "She's just looking for attention, she knows I'm joking!"[61]

Jimmy's parents were nervous about leaving him home alone while they attended one of Nora's dance competitions in St. Louis, a 3-hour drive from their hometown. Jimmy assured them that he was "grown up enough to handle" himself for three days. Reluctantly, they went to St. Louis. When they returned, they found that Jimmy had not attended school during their absence, and over the weekend had thrown a wild party. Beer cans and cigarette butts littered the larger areas of the house, and all the bathrooms— including the master— smelled of haphazardly cleaned up vomit.

Nothing, however, was as shocking as finding Jimmy in the master bed with *two* college-age girls, passed out from a night of heavy drinking. After the young ladies were asked to leave, Jimmy shrugged his shoulders and said matter-of-factly "What? I'm 17! I don't know what the big deal is."

Nora's room had been completely emptied of its furniture, which the family found scattered throughout the backyard. Dresser drawers full of her clothes were strewn beside the back porch swing, and her desk— full of ongoing school projects and class notes— lay on it's back underneath the tree. Jimmy explained: "We needed a room to rave in."

61 Jimmy betrays his own unconscious goal in his evaluation of Nora: he sees her tears as a bid for attention, and must invalidate them to make sure that she doesn't win that bid. His competitive goal (attention) has blinded him to his sister's hurt feelings.

It was also discovered that Nora's makeup products were used to write inappropriate messages on the bathroom mirror and shower door. "It'll come off! It's just a little lipstick, who cares?"

For hours, his parents lectured him on the importance of trust, responsibility, respect, and the "direction" of his life. When asked if he understood what they were saying, Jimmy invariably replied with "I don't know," causing further exasperation— and lecturing.[62]

Jimmy's parents, at their wits' end, determined that it was time to get Jimmy some help from a counselor. They expected resistance from Jimmy, but instead, found him quite amenable to the suggestion. He even suggested that he find his own therapist using an online search tool. His choice couldn't be argued with, although interestingly, the therapist's website specified that he was a *family* therapist. This struck the parents as odd, but not wanting to stir the pot, they accommodated Jimmy's request and scheduled an appointment.

At the end of his first session with the therapist, Jimmy emerged from the office smiling and calm. Something about his appearance reminded his parents of his younger years, when they had their "Happy Jimmy." The therapist

62 Jimmy's parents think that they are "letting him have it." But, Jimmy is winning a competition all throughout their lecture. More than anything else, he wants to win their attention and investment over Nora. As unpleasant as the lecture may be, he has accomplished his goal.

requested to speak with the parents for a few moments, noting that Jimmy had consented to this. The parents sat down and answered some basic questions about how things were going. The therapist seemed genuinely interested and compassionate, expressing a sense of understanding of how difficult things must have been for them the past few years.

"I asked to speak with you, because I'd like to extend an invitation to the whole family to participate in Jimmy's work with me."

The parents looked at each other nervously, but nodded. "Whatever we have to do as parents, we'll do it. We usually are free on Wednesdays and Thursdays, but we can make Friday work too...."

The therapist nodded in appreciation. "And what about Nora? It sounds like she's got a busy schedule; when would she be available to join?"

Both parents were confused. "Well, she is really busy. I'm not sure why Nora would need to be here. She's no trouble at all for us; she and Jimmy don't get along very well, it's true, but really that's mostly Jimmy's fault. He's really mean to her, and I just don't really think it would be necessary for her to be here."

The therapist nodded again in understanding. "I hear what you're saying; it's a little confusing for you— especially given how little trouble Nora gives you— that I might want her to come. Obviously, I am happy to work with whoever comes. But, I do think Nora would be a powerful addition to the group. Would it be helpful if I explained my reasoning?"

"Definitely."

"Well, I think that— in large part— Jimmy's unpleasant and inappropriate behavior is an expression of his discouragement about himself in relation to Nora. You can imagine that for Jimmy, it's tough to be matched up against Nora. From what I hear, she's well put-together. His discouragement doesn't excuse any of his behavior, but if we were able to explore that relationship further, I think we could understand what's going on with Jimmy.

"Some of this might still be a little confusing for you both, and it might be confusing for Nora. I would invite you to bring Nora to at least one appointment. I think that will help with the confusion."

Jimmy's parents agreed to the "test run," but remained skeptical. Why on earth would Nora be part of the problem? She mostly kept to herself; she even responded to Jimmy's cruelest insults with grace and patience. Jimmy really hadn't even talked to her in months. When they asked Jimmy about Nora attending the next appointment, he said that he thought it was strange too. "I didn't even say much about her." Nora— ever the willing participant— agreed to come. "Anything to help Jimmy" she said, earning her an indignant, raised middle finger from Jimmy.

At the next session, the therapist gathered the whole family together. He asked the parents to share when Jimmy's behavior problems had started.

Dad: *Probably seventh grade.*
Mom: *No, it was earlier than that; probably fourth grade? Ms. Wilson had a really tough time with him*

that year.

Jimmy: *Yeah, but remember in third grade I got sus-pended?*

Dad: *That's true; and actually, the more I think about it, I think there were lots of issues going on before school started at all. Remember how we were wor-ried about sending him to preschool because he was having so much trouble at home with us? It turned out just fine, but we were pretty worried because things at home were pretty bad.*

Therapist: *It sounds like things have been tough for a long while.*

Mom: *Yeah, really since he was three or four. It's been a long time.*

Therapist: *What was happening around that time of life for Jimmy?*

Dad: *Well, he was home with us. I was working at the plant back then, but really my schedule was the same. We lived in a different neighborhood, but I don't think that seems very important. I don't know, it felt like things were just...*normal *for him!*

Therapist: *Nora, what do you think was going on for Jimmy around that time?*

Nora: *I don't know. I mean, I could guess, but I really don't know because I had just been born.*

Therapist: *You'd just been born. That's interesting. What do you think* that *was like for Jimmy?*

Nora: *I don't understand. What do you mean?*

Therapist: *I mean, what do you think it was like to be*

Jimmy when you were born?

Nora: *I really don't know!*

Therapist: *That's ok, Nora; it's a tough question. Maybe we could ask Jimmy, since he's probably the authority on the subject! Jimmy— what was it like?*

Jimmy: *It's kind of hard to remember.*

Therapist: *It was a long time ago. Could you share the earliest memory that you have of life?*

Jimmy: *Ok. Let me think. Now that you ask, I have this memory from right after Nora was born. It was right after we came home from the hospital with her. I remember, we are all sitting in the living room, and the house lost power. And I was scared because my parents couldn't see me anymore. And Nora started crying, and my parents started freaking out, because they knew she needed a new diaper but they couldn't find one in the dark. And then I started crying.*

Mom: *That's not what happened, Jimmy. I...*

Therapist: *Mom, I hear you saying you remember it differently. That's ok, of course. If we could, I'd invite all of us to stick with how Jimmy remembers it, even if no one else remembers that way. Would that be ok, even if just for a few minutes?*

Mom: *Sure, I can do that.*

Therapist: *Thanks, mom. Now Jimmy, when you think back on this memory, what is the emotion that sticks out?*

Jimmy: *Um, I think probably...lonely? I don't know,*

that doesn't make sense, 'cause I was with everyone.

Therapist: *Maybe it doesn't make logical sense to you, but it* feels *like the right choice of words?* (Jimmy nods). *Ok, well then let's stick with it, even if it doesn't make sense. For you, Jimmy, what would be the exact opposite of lonely for you? No right or wrong answers.*

Jimmy: *This is weird, but I think the word that comes to mind is "special"?*

Therapist: *That doesn't seem weird to me at all, Jimmy. It sounds like you really wanted to feel special in that moment, and instead you felt lonely.* (Jimmy gets very quiet, and his bottom lip trembles). *That seems to be pretty powerful, for you, Jimmy.*

Jimmy: (After a few moments of silence) *Honestly, that's what it's felt like for a long time. I try so hard to be noticed and special, and to prove myself, and I feel like no matter what I do, you guys [to his parents] are so focused on Nora, that I can't do enough.*

Mom: *That's not true, Jimmy. I can't believe you would say...*

Therapist: *Mom, sorry to interrupt. I can imagine that's hard for you to hear, and it's understandable that you'd like to stick up for yourself. I wonder if we could stick with what Jimmy feels for a bit. I know that's going to be hard, but I think we can do it together.* (Mom nods). *Jimmy, that's a lot of pain you carry around with you. I'm sitting over here wondering how you must have dealt with all that pain.*

Jimmy: *I don't know. I think I have kind of resented Nora. Well, not kind of; I've been really mean to her for a long time, because I don't like how she's always the "Main Attraction."*

Therapist: *Jimmy, for you, what is the exact opposite of "Main Attraction?"*

Jimmy: *Unimportant.*

Therapist: *Wow. That's powerful. Jimmy, we all want to belong in a way where we feel important, so feeling unimportant must have really hurt. It reminds me of what you said about wanting to feel "special." I'm wondering if you also meant "important?"* (Jimmy becomes very tearful and nods). *Yeah, that's very painful. Jimmy, thank you for sharing that with all of us. That took courage.*

Jimmy: *Well, I didn't really mean to!* (Laughing). *It makes a lot of sense now.*

Therapist: **(To everyone)** *What else do you notice about the memory?*

Jimmy: *i don't know. The rest seems pretty normal to me.*

Nora: *Yeah, I don't know either.* (Mom and Dad nod and shrug their shoulders).

Therapist: *Would you all like to hear some things I notice about the memory, so we can make sense of them together?* (Everyone nods). *Ok, so one thing I noticed is that the house lost power. That makes some sense, I think, because when a new sibling comes along, older children often feel a loss of* *power. Sometimes we call it "dethronement," because they've gone from the center of attention to the margins of the family life. Does that make any sense? (Everyone nods). I also notice that what seems most bothersome to Jimmy in the memory is that he's* **not seen**. *Jimmy, I'm wondering: when* **do** *you feel seen by others?*

***Jimmy**: Well, not really ever.*

***Therapist**: Jimmy, I hear a lot of discouragement. I'm also wondering if perhaps you are underestimating how often you're seen. Mom, dad— how much time and energy do you spend* **seeing** *Jimmy?*

***Dad**: It feels like we're constantly watching Jimmy. He's always getting into trouble, and it can be exhausting. We always have to keep an eye on him.*

***Therapist**: Ah, yes. I think I see something. It sounds to me like Jimmy is seen quite a lot, but mostly when things are going poorly.*

***Jimmy**: Yeah, that's right. It's like they see me, but only when I'm doing bad stuff. Nora gets all the attention for good stuff.*

***Therapist**: Yeah, I see that it feels that way to you. So here's what occurs to me: it's always been very important to you to be seen. When you're not seen, you don't feel special or— more accurately—* **important**. *You feel on the outside, forgotten. Now, let's go back to the memory: what do you do in response to being on the outside?*

***Mom**: He cries.*

Therapist: *That's right. He cries. Now mom, tell me how a 17-year-old Jimmy cries to try to be seen and avoid being forgotten.* (Mom becomes very tearful, tries to respond, but can't). *Wow, it seems like that question brings up something pretty powerful for you. If, and when, you're ready, I'd love to hear about it.*
Mom: *All this is making sense to me now. He just felt put to the side, and he is just trying to get back in the picture. And it makes me so sad to think that the only way he feels like he can do that is to be bad. I think that's how he's crying out to us now, by being bad so we* have *to pay attention.*
Therapist: *That's quite an insight. I see Jimmy nodding at what you said, and he looks surprised and thankful to me. Do you see that too? I'm wondering the last time you saw that on his face?* (All family members, aside from Nora, become tearful and quiet). *I think it's probably been a long time. I sense relief, even if just in this moment. I am so thankful for this moment too! Now, Nora, I see now you're a bit on the outside. You seem a little disturbed.*
Nora: *I don't know what to say. I don't really know what I'm feeling right now.* (Silence). *I think I feel kind of defensive? I didn't know I was causing so many problems. I feel bad.*
Therapist: *Nora, that makes a lot of sense, especially with us discussing this early memory of Jimmy's. Maybe you can tell me, what for you is the exact opposite*

of feeling defensive?

Nora: *Probably...defended.*

Therapist: *Jimmy, could you defend Nora for us?* (Everyone looks surprised).

Jimmy: *Me?* (Therapist nods). *Ok. Hmm. I guess, the thing is, it's not Nora's fault. Like, she was just a baby. I don't really know what else she was supposed to do. And really since then, she's done what she's supposed to do. It's not her fault that she's good at everything, it's not her fault that people like her, it's not her fault that she's pretty.* (Nora begins to cry). *The truth is...I think it's all my fault.* (Jimmy's lip starts to quiver).

Therapist: *That's very heavy, Jimmy. Nora, I'm wondering, could you defend Jimmy right now?*

Nora: *Yes. Absolutely. Jimmy, it's not all your fault. I think we've all made the family a pretty tough place for you to be. It's like...we've all had a little bit of an easier time painting you as the bad guy, just 'cause that was more obvious. But I think now I see that you aren't bad. I mean you've been* really *mean* (everyone laughs), *but I think now I see how much you were just trying to be a part of things.*

Therapist: *Jimmy, what is it like to have Nora stick up for you like that?*

Jimmy: *It's...weird?* (Everyone laughs). *But not in a bad way. It honestly feels so good. It's like, for the first time ever, she's on my side.*

Therapist: *Yeah, I imagine that does feel good. And*

what did it feel like to be on her side?
***Jimmy**: It felt good too, but weird* (everyone laughs again). *It felt...*(Jimmy becomes emotional).
***Therapist**: Jimmy, I'm going to make a guess what you were about to say. I think you probably wanted to say "It felt like I was doing something important, like I was a part of the family again."* (Jimmy nods, becoming openly tearful).

At this point in the session, the therapist observed that time was almost up. He thanked them for their courage, honesty, and willingness to work together. When he requested that the entire family return for the next session, everyone nodded enthusiastically.

In subsequent sessions, the therapist was able to help Jimmy further explore his primary mistake: namely, that he had to outshine Nora in order to be seen and belong. Everyone worked together to encourage Jimmy, observing his strengths and helping find ways to put them to use for the family. One session was particularly powerful, in which Jimmy learned that he had unconsciously targeted Nora's "tender spots" in order to enact revenge on her for taking his place of prominence in the family.

Heartbroken at this realization, he asked: "What do I do with that now? I get so tempted to hurt her because I'm so good at it." The therapist observed that Jimmy could be of good service to his sister, advocating for her and respectfully defending her from hurts and offenses directed at her "tender spots." Jimmy wasn't sure when such an opportunity would present itself, as he saw himself as the primary source of hurt for Nora.

He didn't have to wait long for a chance to put his knowledge to use. After one of Nora's dance recitals (the first that Jimmy had ever attended), he overheard a classmate of Nora's commenting about how she looked in a leotard, calling her "very fuck-able."

"Hey, that's my sister. Don't talk about her like that. She's not a piece of meat."

The classmate responded, "It was a compliment! I was saying she looks hot!"

"How she looks isn't anything for you to talk about. If I hear you talking like that again about her or anyone on her team, you're going to have to deal with me."

Nora and her parents walked up at the end of this conversation, and asked what was going on, quite concerned that Jimmy had perhaps started an argument (although choosing to believe the best of him, as they had learned in family therapy). Jimmy just said "That asshole wasn't talking right about Nora, so I set him straight." Nora promptly wrapped her arms around him, and squeezed for almost a full minute.

Jimmy— who thought himself the only devil in Nora's life— didn't know that this boy had been harassing Nora for weeks, making lewd comments about her breasts and other body features.

Jimmy, in this moment, felt incredibly *important*. Nora, who later (privately, away from mom and dad's listening ears) explained the situation to Jimmy and thanked him for his defense, also felt connected and important. Mom and dad, who were watching a total transformation in Jimmy, felt honored by their children's care for one another.

Jimmy still smoked, but less frequently and never inside. His grades improved dramatically— almost inexplicably— as he turned his attention away from his inability to outshine Nora's academic performance and towards his own capabilities. He and Nora occasionally got in arguments, but were able to resolve them without undue harm to the other in the process. Jimmy stopped trying to prove his superiority by asserting his "grown-upness," developing friendships with age-appropriate friends and leaving behind his hard-partying habits. Jimmy's parents spent ample time celebrating his accomplishments, even if and when they paled in comparison to Nora's. After all, it wasn't a competition. The whole family understood that now.

The family determined that they were ready to finish their work with the therapist, who agreed wholeheartedly, seeing that cooperative goals had come to define their interactions as a family.

The Pitfalls of Sibling Relationships (Cain & Abel)

The first sibling pair in the biblical narrative are the infamous Cain and Abel. While growing up, they find different roles in their family and community. Abel becomes a shepherd-rancher, and Cain becomes a farmer. In respect for their Creator, they offer sacrifices from the fruits (or lambs) of their labor. Without much explanation,[63] we are told that God accepts Abel's sacrifice, but has "no regard" for Cain's.

Cain becomes angry. In view of social adaptation, anger is the *obstacle removal emotion* (Rasmussen, 2010). It is the emotion that effectively energizes us to remove what is prohibitively in between us and what we desire. God sees Cain's anger and speaks to him, pointing out that he can— without any change in Abel— receive acceptance if he (Cain) would only "do well." God also offers a warning, noting that sin is crouching at Cain's door, and its desire is to master him. God follows this with an invitation for Cain to "rule over" his sin, an observation of Cain's *choice* in the matter.

Cain unfortunately does not heed God's warning about sin, nor His invitation to make a proper choice that would result in gaining acceptance from God. Instead, Cain directs his anger at what he *thinks* is the obstacle to God's acceptance: not his own wrongdoing, but his brother Abel. Cain invites Abel out into a field and murders him, symbolically removing the obstacle to his Heavenly Father's acceptance and "regard." Tragically (but predictably), he receives no such regard, and instead his brother's blood speaks from the ground a "word of condemnation" over Cain.

Whatever we believe about the Bible, this is indisputably an archetypal story of sibling dynamics.

---

63 It is not fair to say that there is no explanation for this difference. We do learn that Abel offered the "firstborn of his flock, and of their fat portions," while Cain simply brings an "offering of the fruit of the ground." Abel's sacrifice appears to be more costly, and therefore valuable and indicative of greater dedication and thankfulness to his Creator.

1. Siblings find their "niches."

2. One niche is perceived to be preferred by the parent(s) or authority.[64]

3. One of two possibilities occurs: a) The non-preferred sibling discovers that a meaningful place of belonging is available, even without being the favorite. If this occurs, the cycle of sibling conflict is disrupted. b) The non-preferred sibling perceives the superior/preferred sibling as the obstacle to their desired state. In this case, the sibling continues in the conflict cycle.

4. Jealousy, envy, anger, and discouragement are born and nourished in the sibling who perceives themselves to be in the "one down" position.

5. These emotions are expressed in a way that, whether literally or symbolically, remove the preferred sibling from the competitive field.

6. Rather than resulting in the desired state, the aggressor finds themself in a new niche: they are given the title of "Bad One," further exacerbating their feelings of inferiority. The aggressor returns to Step 1.

7. The cycle repeats in perpetuity, **unless interrupted at Step 3a** *by the non-preferred sibling finding a meaningful place of belonging.*

---

64 This perception can in fact be accurate, but doesn't have to be to exert power over a person's emotions or choices. Many children who are— in fact— the "favorite" perceive the other sibling(s) to be favored. It should also be mentioned that *most* parents, in spite of all their protests, do have and play favorites. Their denials are simply an attempt to avoid the responsibility and pain of the realization, both for parent and child. It's notable that children, joyfully unencumbered by social demands for acceptable dishonesty, almost ubiquitously agree that parents play favorites.

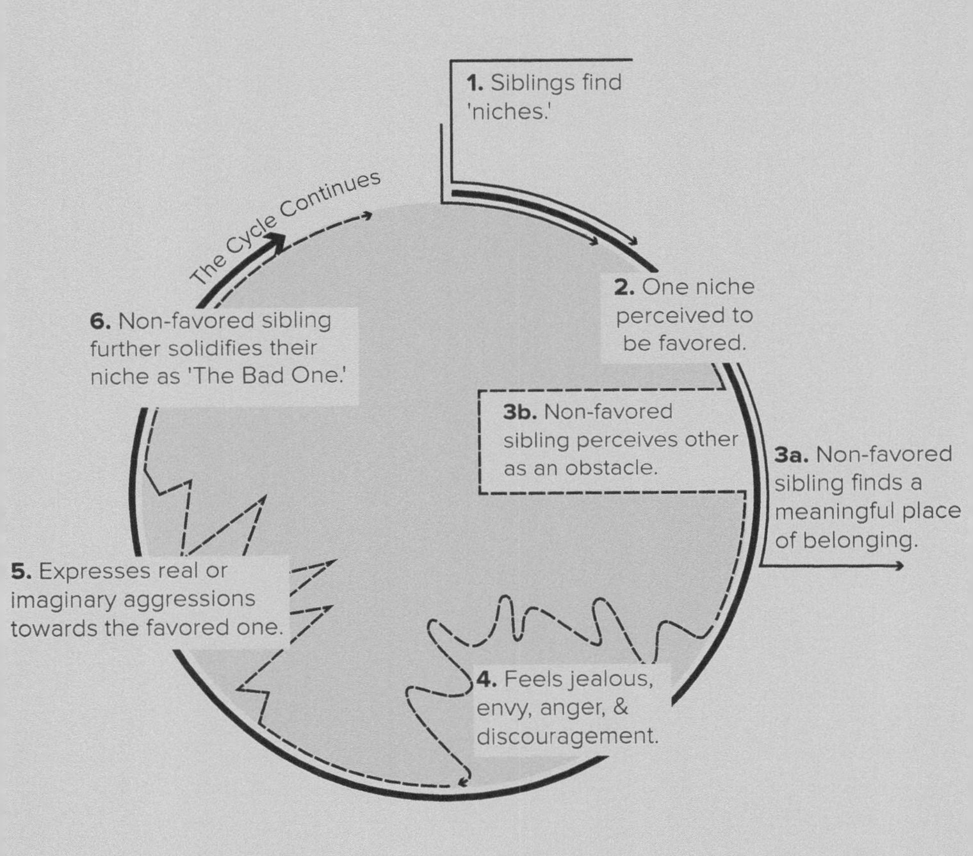

Cycle of Sibling Conflict

This archetypal story is played out among siblings all over the world. While practices like economic primogeniture[65] have— in large part— been extinguished in the developed world, humanity has not done away with sibling-centric envy and anger. Rather, we have increased our sensitivity to slights, favoritism, acceptance, and parental "regard." It may not be the inheritance of the family acreage that alerts us to favoritism, but instead the decision by parents to allow one child to sleepover at a friend's house at the age of 8, but allow another at the age of 7. These perceptions of inferiority-superiority dynamics are wholly unavoidable. Adler stated that to be human "is to possess feelings of inferiority." Nonetheless, it is a challenge we must face with serious, focused courage.

The archetypal cycle described above is a competition: "Who Will Gain the Favor of the Powers-That-Be?" It is no accident that the Bible regularly describes God as a Father. Parents are symbolic representations of God: powerful, responsible for our creation, seemingly all-knowing. Therefore, the Cain and Abel story— and what it represents archetypally— is functionally about gaining the *sole and unfettered* "regard" of a parent, and the competition that ensues when this is our goal. It assumes a specific kind of social scarcity: *There can only be one favorite, and whoever isn't the favorite has no place.*

---

65 Primogeniture was an economic practice in which inheritance was passed from parents exclusively to a first-born child (historically, a first-born male child).

Common Battlegrounds

While our sensitivity to parental or authoritative "regard" takes almost limitless forms, certain competitions are extremely common among siblings.

- *Who is the best behaved?*
- *Who is the least trouble?*[66]
- *Who is the funniest?*
- *Who commands the most attention?*
- *Who is the smartest?*
- *Who is the wittiest?*
- *Who is the most mature?*
- *Who is the most athletic?*
- *Who is oldest/biggest?*
- *Who is the toughest?*
- *Who is most handsome/beautiful?*
- *Who does mom/dad spend the most time with?*
- *Who is in charge?*
- *Who needs/gets the most help?*
- *Who is the most successful?*[67]

66 A wholly different competition from "who is the best behaved?" High achievers are often high-maintenance individuals; sometimes lower achievers can "win regard" by flying under the radar and being little to no trouble.
67 What is deemed "successful" varies from family to family. In one family, success may be measured by academics. In another, it may be measured in athletic achievement. In another, maintaining a heterosexual orientation may be the sign of success, or lifelong (and strict) adherence to a religion. Some families may even consider impoverished misery to be a sign of success: "You didn't get won-over by those rich snobs."

- *Who works the hardest/least?*
- *Who gets the most desirable chores?*
- *Who gets away with undesirable behavior more often?*

The trouble with these competitions is that they often work quite well for us. Some reduce the frequency and severity of negative consequences for "bad" behavior. Others earn us laughter and well-wishes from those around us. Some get us jobs and positions of prominence, or keep bullies away. Others earn us the affection and adoration of peers, even romantic attention and sex. They result in steady and (sometimes) substantial income, and they protect us from some of the more unpleasant responsibilities of life. So much about these competitions appears good to us, and they appear *especially* good to our parents. What parent would complain about a child who is well-behaved? Successful? Tough? Easy-to-manage? Smart?

How could a parent punish such things?

These questions only further illustrate the dangerous nature of behavior-based home environments that depend solely on reward and punishment as the tools of child-rearing: *The best behaviors can come from the worst character*. If a child makes straight A's, is that a good thing or a bad thing? Behaviorally, straight A's are indisputably good. However, if we find that the child uses those grades to shame and belittle a younger sibling or other proto-siblings[68] at school, can we still call the grades "good?" If a child's excellent performance is precious to them because it can be weaponized against others, is it still desirable?

Families must learn to identify competitive goals and subordinate them to cooperative goals. What Cain failed to see in his brother Abel was a successful rancher who could put meat on the table for the whole family, not to mention the provision of fertilizer for his crops. A cooperative opportunity was right in front of him: "How can we flourish together?" If Cain had been able to subordinate any competition to this goal, he would have been able to"do well and be accepted." Instead, he failed to root out the competitive goal ("I must not be second to anyone"), and lost his right to participate in the most ancient of all communities: the family.

While most of us won't suffer literal exile as punishment for our competitive striving, we will— in a very real way— lose a sense of belonging and connection with our families if we insist on competing with them.

Identifying Competition Among Siblings

How *do* we identify competitive goals? An old saying suggests that "The proof of the pudding is in the eating of it." Meaning: it's hard to know whether something is good or bad until it's experienced. Within the context of sibling relationships, one question can serve as a litmus test to determine whether siblings are striving horizontally or vertically: when one child does well, do the other siblings genuinely celebrate it?"

---

68 By virtue of close contact and similar age, schoolmates functionally serve as siblings outside of the home.

Families should be on the lookout for certain behaviors that may indicate a lack of celebration:

- *"One-upping" a sibling ("Oh yeah? Well one time I....")*
- *Undermining accomplishments ("That's not that hard! Big whoop.").*
- *Changing the subject ("Can we talk about something else now?").*
- *Isolating, excusing oneself from the celebration (This may take the form of somatic complaints; e.g., a stomach- or head-ache, fatigue, dizziness.).*
- *Silence or lack of responsiveness; withdrawing socially or emotionally.*
- *Particularizing accomplishments to the individual alone ("Good for them, I guess!"[69]).*
- *Taking credit for accomplishments ("I helped them study for that test, so it's kind of my A+ too!").*

Siblings who are ultimately cooperative in their relationship with siblings will feel dignified and pleased at the success of their brothers and sisters, which would render most of the above responses useless and nonsensical. To undermine or minimize the significance of a sibling's success only serves to minimize positive feeling for a cooperative family, as the mindset of the family is one of "rising tides raise all boats." Why would a truly cooperative sibling hold the

69 Possible implication: "Not good for me."

metaphorical tide at bay? Only a competitive goal would make the behaviors described above useful.

One other question could be asked of a group of siblings as a way to identify competition: "When a child fails or suffers, do the other siblings celebrate it?" To answer "yes" is not an accusation of sadism or sociopathy in siblings. On the contrary, as often as competition between siblings can be found, we find children celebrating the suffering and failure of their siblings.

Some forms of celebration are less obvious than others. Here are some typical ways in which children show their pleasure in a sibling's suffering:

- *Laughing at another's pain or failure ("Ha, look what he did!").*
- *Tattling*[70] *("Dad, she just threw the truck at Steven!")*
- *Watching or "listening in" on a rebuke or consequence (E.g., Standing outside the door when a child is put in time-out or punished.).*
- *Reminding family members or peers of mistakes*[71] *("Remember when Claire got a bad grade on her spelling test?").*

---

70 There are appropriate times to alert an adult or authority figure to misconduct, especially in moments where safety is in question. However, there is a meaningful distinction between this appropriate behavior and tattling. The goal of tattling is to get someone else in trouble, and in doing so, to gain the upper hand. Children and adolescents can, contrarily, approach an adult or authority with a cooperative goal: "*We* are having a tough time keeping it together over here, could you help us figure out what to do?"

- *Flaunting privileges that have been taken away from the sibling in trouble ("I'm leaving to go out with my friends now. I'm glad I'm not grounded!").*
- *Meddling in others' unpleasant business ("So wait, she dumped you right in front of your friends? I need details.").*
- *Failure to courageously advocate for or defend their sibling ("Hey, it's not my problem those kids were picking on him. What did you want* **me** *to do?").*
- *Rescuing the sibling through codependency or pity*[72] *("Poor Stephanie, come to your big sister and I'll make it all better.").*

If a sibling is interested in cooperation, these responses to difficulty and suffering in another are useless and senseless. Instead of relishing, reminding, or "repeating a matter," cooperative siblings overlook[73], encourage, and empathize.

71 These reminders can, at times, sound quite empathetic and caring: "I just keep thinking about how Scott hit that other kid at school; I just don't know how he could do that, it doesn't *sound* like Scott at all. He's so sweet and gentle!" If said once or twice, it may indicate an appropriate concern; if repeated ad nauseam, it's likely that the sibling is attempting— consciously or otherwise— to put Scott in a "one down" position by reminding others of his poor choice.

72 Pity might look virtuous and caring, but this could not be further from the truth. Pity is deeply disrespectful, as it communicates to another: "You're just too helpless and broken to be of any use; I'll heroically save you!" Pity is competitive striving masquerading as care and concern.

73 There is a kind of "overlooking" that is unhelpful: namely, one that makes a mistake or painful experience more likely to reoccur. However, overlooking small missteps and avoiding obsession over painful experiences can be helpful in framing these moments in the bigger picture.

Helping Siblings Become Cooperative

Individuals in competitive families may feel overwhelmed and discouraged by the immense challenge of rooting out competition. Identifying the competitions is only the first step. Once identified, they must be replaced with cooperative goals. A competitive goal is not *easily* replaced, but it can be *simply*[74] replaced by habitually engaging in a step-wise process:

1. Identify competition where it exists and name it.

The section above highlights some specific ways to become aware of competitive striving among siblings. Naming it, however, requires some tact. When competition is called out, it should only ever be done empathetically, and in solidarity with the competitive individuals. It would be senseless to stir up further feelings of inferiority by using shame or rebuke to verbally identify competition.

> *"Look at yourself, you're competing again— just like always! What is wrong with you?"*

Such a tactic will only exacerbate the problem. Competition springs from feelings of inferiority, so making those feelings even stronger will only serve to intensify competition.

---

74 Simple is different than easy. Simplicity describes the relative complexity of a task; ease describes the extent to which the completion of a task is uninhibited by existing motivations, habits, or level of competence.

> *"Hey buddy, it feels like you're trying to show me that you're better than your sister at that game. Sometimes I do that: trying to one-up somebody else."*

This response, while not perfect, illustrates an empathetic and respectful response. It isn't a "pet theory" of the parent, as it leaves room for the son to correct the parent's observation. It builds solidarity, as the parent admits to competing themselves. Naming a competition in this way invites awareness, but without increasing the likelihood that competition will be intensified by putting another in a one-down, inferior position.

2. Empathize with the inferiority feeling behind the competition.

Now that a baseline awareness of competitive striving has been developed, the *actual cause* of the striving must be identified. A great deal of specificity isn't necessarily needed in this step. Something as simple as "I'd imagine you don't feel very good right now" can go a long way. Family members should never excuse behavior in this step, nor should they insist that the competing sibling accept the intuition of inferiority feelings.

> *"Sean, chill out. Your sister Beth only hit you because she feels terrible about her body. Cut her a break!"*

Beth's feelings of inferiority do not offer her the right to hit her brother, nor can anyone be certain of how she feels about her body.[75]

"Hey Beth, I see you just hit Sean. I don't think he liked that very much. I'm thinking that you probably aren't feeling very good right now; can you tell me about it so we can all understand?"

In this response, Beth isn't let off the hook, nor is she demeaned. Instead, she is directed to the actual problems: 1) she behaved in a divisive manner that hurt her relationship with Sean, and 2) she feels quite terrible, even after hitting Sean. She's confronted, but with a desire for relationship and understanding. This is crucial, as most inferiority feelings are— in the larger sense— rooted in a dread that we don't *belong with significance*. If— even in a moment of confrontation— Beth get's the message "You belong here, you have a place, it's important to us what's going on with you," she is invited to adopt a cooperative stance towards her family members.

3. Reorient towards cooperation.

People don't change their behavior (or, more importantly, their character!) by being shown that their current faults are "bad:" they change when they adopt a new and better goal. Educator Sir Richard Livingstone (1954) wrote "One is apt to think of moral failure as due to weakness of character: more often it is due to an inadequate ideal" (153). The competing sibling

---

75 Although, after such a statement being made in her presence, it's unlikely that Beth would feel positively about her body!

possesses the inadequate goal of defeating of a rival sibling. To change, they must be won over to a better ideal.

Thomas Chalmers (1846), in his infamous sermon entitled "The Expulsive Power of a New Affection," made an insightful observation about what helps human beings to change.

> *"...If the way to disengage the heart from the positive love of one great and ascendant object, is to fasten it in positive love to another, then it is not by exposing the worthlessness of the former, but by addressing to the mental eye the worth and excellence of the latter, that all old things are to be done away and all things are to become new" (274).*

In other words, people are won over from something old (competition) to something new (cooperation) not by being shown the faults of their current "way," but by seeing— in all its splendor— a new and better way of doing things (cooperation). The competing sibling must see both 1) the reality of the opportunity to cooperate, and 2) the real and tangible benefits of cooperation with their sibling. This reorientation cannot be forced, nor is it didactic. Reorientation is— not coincidentally— a *cooperative* endeavor. A family member wishing to help siblings cooperate cannot use force or bribery, as this would hypocritically model competitive striving.[76]

---

76 Force and bribery say to another person: "I have the requisite power and resources to make you do what I want."

"Joey, I'm sick and tired of all the fighting. Aren't you sick of it too? It's awful being around here, with all the yelling between you and Nick. Enough already!"

This response does an excellent job of exposing the unpleasantries of Joey and Nick's competition. But, what does it win Joey *over to*? Joey knows what he's not supposed to do. But, he might ask— internally— "What now? What else am I to do?" Joey, though he is mistaken, feels that the only options available to him are to defeat Nick in every competition possible, or to be relegated to a chronic position of inferiority. The first option costs Joey his comfort, his friendship with Nick, and the temporary pleasure of his parents. The second option costs Joey his dignity and place in the home, a cost *vastly* larger than that of the first option.

"Joey, I wonder if you know that we're so happy you're in our family, whether or not you win this argument with Nick. You belong here, and you're important. I wonder, Joey— if you felt that way, what might you do with Nick today to build friendship instead of fighting?"

This response *truly* comforts Joey, because it attends to his greatest fear— failing to belong in a way that matters. It also wins Joey's cooperation by encouraging *him* to find the solution, rather than prescribing one. Joey, if he feels that his place of belonging and significance is secure, is now free to "expel" the competitive goal and lay hold of a better outcome through a cooperative endeavor: friendship with Nick.

If Joey fails to come up with a solution, a helping family member should be wary of finding one for him.[77] Rather, a cooperative and encouraging response might sound like this:

> *"It's a tough question. I'd be happy to talk it through with you, but maybe you need more time. Either way, let me know if I can help. I'm sure you'll figure it out. I love you!"*

Joey continues to feel that cooperation is— in fact— a possible avenue, and that there is something to be gained by pursuing it.

4. Notice and encourage cooperative motivations and behavior.

So much of building good habits is mindful celebration of the benefits of those good habits. After I exercise, I take a moment to really *notice* the endorphins pumping through my body. When I wake up after going to bed at a decent hour the night before, I take stock of how good it feels to be rested. These mindful moments solidify my movement towards healthy discipline, and failing to take them often results in a crumbling commitment to doing what is best. The same is true for cooperation. If families only confront competitiveness but never celebrate or enjoy cooperation, it is unlikely that said family will maintain cooperative goals.

77 It is often through well-intended help, not malicious insult, that we discourage others. To habitually do for another what they can do for themselves is disrespect dressed in the trappings of "helpfulness." It communicates to another: "You can't handle this challenge, so now I have to do it for you."

It should be noted that celebration can be easily undermined by "yes, but..." observations by others.

> *"Wow Paul— you really helped your sister! I wish you had done it earlier, but still, good job!"*

Paul will most likely hear and remember *only* the criticism. He'll walk away frustrated and feeling put down, since the overarching message is: "You didn't measure up." Additionally, Paul may be given the sense that the primary advantage of cooperation was to hear a word of approval ("Good job!") from a family member. This is *not* the primary advantage of cooperation. Paul wins friendship and reaffirms his significance in the family by helping, and benefits from the overall flourishing of the group.

> *"Paul, I love how you helped your sister just then. It seems like that meant a lot to her. How are you feeling after showing kindness?"*

This response notices Paul's cooperative action, accurately identifies its significance, and invites him to decide for himself what the benefits are. Even if Paul is young and can only articulate that he "feels good," he is not missing the big picture: Helping is necessary, helping feels good, helping makes things go well for everyone.

It should be noted that the above suggestions can be implemented by parents *or* siblings. In fact, it's probable that if and when *siblings* implement these steps, the sibling group

Addressing Sibling Competition

STEP 1:

Identify and name competition.

STEP 2:

Empathize with the feeling behind the competition.

STEP 3:

Reorient towards cooperation.

STEP 4:

Notice/Encourage cooperative movements and goals.

• *Don't confuse naming with blaming.* • *Beware of pet theories; start with "Could it be that...?"* • *Stay away from the competition of "Who is best at naming the competition we are in?"*	• *Build solidarity through humility.* • *Affirm belonging and importance at all times.* • *Look for group ownership of the competition, not a scape goat.*
• *Don't worry about being insightful; simple empathy works just fine.* • *Never excuse inappropriate or uncooperative behavior.* • *Avoid insisting on a competing party accepting your empathic observations.*	• *See the discouragement instead of the behavior alone.* • *Invite responsibility for actions that doesn't infer inferiority from mistakes.* • *Attend to relational challenges rather than behavior missteps.*
• *Don't try to motivate through guilt, shame or fear - you will be unsuccessful.* • *Beware of prohibitions without alternatives.* • *Avoid over-prescribing solutions; start by asking competitors for their ideas.*	• *Reassure siblings with their unwavering opportunity to belong with significance.* • *Point siblings toward the natural rewards of cooperation.* • *Encourage collaborative problem-solving instead of unilateral strategies.*
• *Avoid exception clauses (e.g., "Yes, but...") that focus on the negative.* • *Use encouragement instead of praise (see Chapter 4).* • *Don't restrict these steps to parents: siblings' participation is vital!*	• *Catch the siblings working together, even in small ways.* • *Ask them what they feel like after cooperating.* • *Maintain respect for siblings; responsibility to maintain a positive relationship with one another.*

will have more success in developing cooperation. While parents can be helpful in rooting out competition and reorienting towards cooperation, it's often the sibling group themselves who are most empowered to make necessary changes. Siblings tend to be the most acutely aware of competitive dynamics. They have a sensitivity to being put in a one-down position that parents could never have, so their "radar" for active competition is more accurate. When siblings take the challenge on, they avoid the possible pitfalls of power struggle between child and parent and learn to take responsibility for their own relationships.

Conclusion

The importance of sibling relationships in the development of cooperative capacity cannot be overstated. Siblings are— in essence— our first peer group, and because of their relative equality with us, they are also the people with whom we are most likely to compete. If and when siblings compete, there are only two options: win, and in the process subject the other sibling(s) to feelings of inferiority that inevitably result in compensatory action; or lose, and become increasingly discouraged about the prospect of managing the challenges of life. When siblings cooperate instead of competing, they learn what is— arguably— *the* essential skill of social living: They find a place of belonging through contribution to the well-being of a group.

6

Intergenerational Competition & Cooperation: A Brief Investigation

A few years ago, I watched a video that a friend had posted on social media entitled "Millennials: We Suck and We're Sorry." The clip humorously catalogs the tongue-in-cheek apologies of several young adults who seem quite sincere, if not self-deprecating. "We're self-centered. We're entitled. We're narcissistic, lazy, and immature. And we're sorry about that."[78]

The apologetic young adults observe that perhaps they should have been more like their parents, the Baby Boomers. Sarcasm defines their observations of Baby Boomer tendencies: counter-cultural attitudes, psychedelic drug use, permissive parenting, and inordinate insistence on college education which has resulted in an average of $30,000

78 At this point in the book, the reader should see the competition that is taking shape. The Millennials in the video are expressing their sense of inferiority in comparison to other generations, and as the self-deprecation intensifies, so does the potential for blowback/compensation.

in student loan debt for graduates. Veiled criticisms eventually give way to all-out accusations, as Boomers are blamed— perhaps fairly, perhaps unfairly— for the outsourcing of the "good jobs," a recession that severely limited economic mobility for young professionals, the death of thousands of young soldiers sent into battle by Boomer politicians voted in by Boomer voters, the gutting of labor unions, and environmental devastation.

Yikes.

It should be noted that the vitriol expressed in the video— however humorous— didn't emerge from a vacuum. Millennials, at the time the clip was produced, were being brutally maligned by politicians, public figures, news outlets, and yes— *older family members*. The Millennial actors/producers were simply compensating for being put repeatedly in an inferior position. Likewise, Boomers' insults were also compensations for their own feelings of inferiority, as their vision for American life was looking more and more impossible. Boomers were themselves maligned in their youth, as have countless generations before them.

The Ubiquitous Error of Intergenerational Competition

Generational competition has been around for millennia. Even the New Testament records competitive attitudes between generations. Jesus, in a list of "woes to the Pharisees," includes this condemnation: "Woe to you, scribes and Pharisees, hypocrites! For you build the tombs of the prophets and decorate the monuments of the righteous, saying 'If we had lived in the days of our fathers, we would not have taken part in shedding the blood of the prophets' " (Matthew 23:29-30, English Standard Version). In other words, the religious elites of Jesus' day were honoring dead prophets by building and maintaining elaborate monuments for them, all the while thinking to themselves "We never would have treated these people so badly; we are clearly better than our ancestors, who murdered them."

The irony of this passage in Matthew is that these same scribes and Pharisees are about to consummate a plot to have Jesus— whom the Bible presents as the Ultimate Prophet— murdered in cold blood.

Current generations persist in this kind of competitive striving. Case in point: modern Americans have dubbed one generation "The Greatest Generation."

Differences between generations are often what we use to put each other down. Younger generations tend to see older generations as "behind the times," technologically illiterate, pompous, unhelpfully conservative, and too attached to tired ideas and methods. They ignore how the efforts and values of older generations have provided them with the freedom to move forward into new territory, and even laid the groundwork for the technology that older folks sometimes struggle to use.

Older generations tend to see younger generations as entitled, lazy, undisciplined, spoiled, and unhelpfully liberal. They fail to acknowledge their creativity and willingness to take advantage of reduced scarcity.

When generations set their sights on maintaining a

superior position over another, we commit (at least) two fatal errors.

First, we blind ourselves to our own faults and shortcomings. Like the scribes and the Pharisees in the New Testament, we fail to recognize that we are often guilty of the exact same faults as the generations for which we have disdain.[79] Some Boomers complain that Millennials are "entitled." Of course, those same Boomers feel entitled to progeny who will behave in a manner they would prefer, include applauding Boomer choices and values. Millennials complain that older generations are too "set in their ways." Yet all-too-often, Millennials refuse to make even small adjustments to better accommodate and serve older generations.

Secondly, we fail to put our differences to *use* for the well-being of all. When we pathologize the traits and values of another group, we will never optimally experience the value of those traits and values. When older generations look down on and shame younger generations for their dependence on technology, they inevitably limit how that technology can be put to use for the global community, *their generation included*. It's unlikely that the grandchild who is constantly berated for being on their phone will go out of their way to help grandma learn to improve her technological

---

79 Jesus observes that a whole host of generations — past and current — had no "taste" for the truth, and were willing to kill to silence those who spoke it.

literacy, which might in turn enable grandma to curtail the maleffects of aging in her ability to manage the daily tasks of living. It's also unlikely that a wise grandparent would make a concerted effort to share wisdom with a grandchild who openly opposes any ideas that are not new and shiny.

The Cost of Competition Between Generations

How many opportunities for human flourishing have been obfuscated by generational competition? This self-inflicted detriment to the global community is incalculable. Competition has inhibited the passing along of abiding wisdom for life, discouraged countless youngsters from putting their skills and perspectives to use for others, created division in families, decreased solidarity in the community-at-large, and marginalized important contributions unnecessarily.

Personally, I can count on one hand the number of older men (age 65+) who have taken an active and prolonged interest in my development as a person. Many, if not most, older men have seemed indifferent or opposed to my contributions, regularly invoking my need to "pay dues" or "get some life experience" before making myself useful. While perhaps well-intentioned, statements like "When you're *my age*, you'll understand __________" have discouraged and belittled me. A competition of "Who is the Oldest?" is being played out, and I— as the younger man— bear the title of "Loser." This only serves to ignite my striving for power over the condescending party.

On the other hand, a few men have given me the

opposite impression: “Calvin, it’s *vital* that you lend a hand right now. You have something to offer, and I want to see you offer it.” It’s not an accident that most of those men— though not all— are the men to whom this book is dedicated.

To be fair, I must admit to having ample disdain for the elderly. My attitude has often been: “Get out of the way, old-timer! It’s *my turn*!” This has put me at odds with people from whom I have much to learn. I have minimized my elders’ contributions by writing them off as luddites and codgers. Whether those judgments were fair or not, I failed to cooperate with them and undeniably am the worse for it, as is my community.

How many opportunities for human flourishing would be available if different generations would develop a cooperative goal? It’s staggering to consider what we could accomplish as a global community if we were to look out for one another, considering everyone a meaningful participant in the human community, regardless of their generation.

Unhampered by discouragement from older generations, what could the young people of the world contribute?

Given the listening ears of the young, what wisdom could the older generations of the world share?

Being regarded as useful, how could the retirees of the world serve the world with their new-found time and availability?

Un-insulted for their youth, what new insights could the creativity of the young discover?

Intergenerational Cooperation

It is nothing short of a tragedy how generational competition has limited our capacity for global flourishing. The question is, how can we work to end this tragedy?

Within the family we can establish precedents for how to manage inter-generational dynamics. Cooperation between generations can be modeled, tested, and encouraged. Competitive goals can be shown to be useless and distasteful if simple steps are taken within families.

1. *Actively spend time outside of your generational "loop."*

It's incredibly difficult to cooperate with others if we are never around them. It's also incredibly easy to maintain uncharitable, competitive attitudes towards people we don't really know. If grandparents spent time with their teenage grandchildren, they would find them to be much more hard-working and motivated than they imagined. If grandchildren spent more time with their grandparents, they would probably find them to be much less curmudgeonly than they imagined. After a year of spending several hours every afternoon with my Papaw, I was surprised to find him quite a bit less conservative and closed-minded than I had assumed. I certainly didn't pull him to a more centrist position: I simply discovered who he was in a more accurate way. Time together creates helpful cognitive dissonance that disabuses us of our close-mindedness about other generations. When our attitudes shift, we are better equipped to cooperate.

2. Strive to see, understand, and communicate the strengths of other generations.

When we are frustrated with the differences we see in another generation, we can choose to recognize the *benefit* of that difference for us and for the community at-large. We can ask ourselves "What would the world be like without that trait or value?" When a young person becomes frustrated with how slowly great-aunt Marie tells a story, they can consider how a community might look if all communication was stripped of pacing and inefficiency. One need only look to Twitter's platform to see the predictable results: increased division and reduced nuance. In this realization, the young person is not necessarily compelled to take on great-aunt Marie's storytelling style as their own. However, they are compelled to acknowledge the social value of Aunt Marie's patient—if not plodding— pattern of speech, no matter how irritating it may be.

3. Avoid condescension of any kind related to generational difference.

There is simply no valid reason to condescend to another person based on their generation. If, indeed, another person's faults need to be addressed, then let them be addressed as faults of choice, rather than the faults of a generation. Rather than saying "Ugh, you're being such a lazy Millennial right now!", we can say "Pete, it seems you've not really been as helpful as you could have been today. Can we talk about that?" Rather than saying "Oh grandma, stop being such a close-minded Boomer!", we can say "Grandma, it feels like you're being pretty judgmental towards me right now. That's not the kind of relationship I want to have; can we find another way to communicate?" What can the young *do* about being young? What can the old *do* about being old? The answer is nothing. It is of no benefit to pathologize and critique what cannot be changed.

4. *Work together on a tough challenge with people outside of your generation.*

The best way to learn *to cooperate* is...well, to cooperate. You can't really know how to ride a bike until you ride a bike, and similarly, it's hard to know how to cooperate with an older or younger generation if you never do it. Admittedly, there are times for generationally homogenous work on life's challenges. However, inter-generational work is incredibly difficult to find, and that says more about our lack of imagination and willingness to cooperate than actual lack of possibility or potential. Why can't a grandfather take on the challenge of painting a bedroom together with a grandchild? Why couldn't a grandson help grandpa pay his bills online?

5. *Avoid unidirectional dynamics in intergenerational relationships; strive for bi-directionality.*

One of the greatest gifts Papaw (my maternal grandfather) gave to me was that he never treated me like a "young buck" *who* only needed to be taught. Of course, he did teach me many things. But just as often, Papaw treated *me* like *his* teacher. He asked me questions about my life, and about things I knew about that he didn't.

I remember standing with him in a shopping mall parking lot. We were waiting for my mom and Mamaw to "finish up in Dillards." (That meant we were probably going to be out there a couple of hours.).

Earlier in the day, he had learned that I was interested in cars. Now in the parking lot, he spent two hours asking me to teach him the makes and models of every car that drove past. He remarked "You know, when I was your age we just had a Ford and a Chevy— I can't believe you know all of these!" He then proceeded to test himself, making guesses about makes and models, and got as excited as a little kid when he guessed correctly.

Papaw taught me all kinds of things (e.g., what an "F1" cow is, the difference between Gramma and Tabosa grass, how to hunt for native American arrowheads, the importance of hard work and kindness). But, it never felt like he had taken me on as a project or student, but rather a partner in living and learning.

Mentorships, apprenticeships, and other unidirectional relationships are needed, undoubtedly. But how often do we unnecessarily conceptualize intergenerational relationships in these ways? How much more often could we create and maintain cooperative friendships across generational lines?

One final note is needed here. While the responsibility for intergenerational cooperation is shared between the young and the old, older generations have a higher imperative of responsibility. It is simply unreasonable to expect young people, who— of no fault of their own!— lack relative brain development, experience, wisdom, and skill, to the make most of the movement. If you're older, you might be thinking: "That's not fair!" Of course, you are correct. But, as older generations are quick to observe to those younger than themselves: "Life isn't fair, is it?" We must pursue cooperation, something more important and satisfying than the pursuit of absolute equity. Those of us who are a bit closer to our graves need to attend to it, rather than engaging in an (ironically) childish game of 'chicken': "I will if they will!"

Conclusion

Like in other interpersonal relationships, we strive to gain a sense of superiority over others outside of our generation. We treat life as a competition to see what generation will "win out" with a "better resume" of traits, values, and accomplishments. Our prize for this victory is— frankly— pitiful: a cheap sense of superiority over a generation which we will soon lose, whether by virtue of death or the contemptuous revenge of those we have defeated. In the process, we lose the chance to learn from and encourage those of different generations for the betterment of humankind. The necessity of improvement on this plane of social living cannot be overstated. We *must* do better to build cooperation between generations.

7

The Stakes

As we arrive at the end of this book, it is worth a few extra pages to consider *why* working on the challenges I've enumerated is worth our effort. Why does it matter if we compete or cooperate?

We might agree that— in its most extreme expression— competition is an inferior approach when compared to cooperation. If *all* we did was compete and we never cooperated, things would clearly be worse. But, that's rarely our experience of life. We often cooperate, and in other moments, we compete. That begs certain questions:

- *What's the problem with a little bit of competition?*
- *Isn't variety the spice of life?*
- *Won't a wholly cooperative way of doing life leave us complacent, weak, or lacking individuality?*
- *Couldn't cooperative living give way to an unhealthy collectivism in which the well-being of individuals are ignored for the well-being of the group?*

These are fair questions that *should* be answered as we consider competitive and cooperative dynamics. Some brief reminders from early chapters are necessary as we attend to the challenge.

The Virtue of Subordinated Competition

First, we must remember that competition is not— in and of itself— pathological. There are clear upsides to competition. Competitive dynamics motivate us, pushing humanity into new territories of competence, excellence, and mastery. Competition helps increase product quality and decrease product price. For this reason, we try — to prevent the presence of monopolies or (supposedly) "cooperative" price-fixing.

Those opposed to competition of any kind are — ironically — embroiled in an intense competition for superiority over others. They give the world a message: "Your competitions seem to me to be hopelessly unfair; therefore, I will hold them in contempt as I play a new game: 'Who is Least Competitive?'"

Secondly, the question is not whether or not we compete. We will. Rather, the question is whether competitive goals reign supreme, or whether *they are subordinated to our cooperative goals.*

I often talk with clients about how there is more than one way to want something. I tell them: "I would love to drive a Ferrari. But, I also want to be free of the hassle, work schedule, career choices, and financial hampering that a Ferrari would cost me. I have two wants that are contradictory. But which desire is greater? Which *kind of wanting* determines whether I have an imported sports car in my driveway?"

Couples tell me "We want to stay together." Individual clients tell me "I want to feel better." Parents tell me "I want to stop fighting with my child." These clients are not *lying* to me by any means, but they also are withholding a higher truth. It is true that they want these things, but they want them *less* than they want other things. The couple wants to stay together, but what they want *most* is to exact revenge on their partner for all slights and injuries. The individual wants to not feel so depressed, but what they want *most* is to conscript others into their service through displays of inadequacy. The parent wants to stop arguing with their child, but what they want *most* is to gain compliance, even if through force.

Cooperative living doesn't require that we abandon all competition. It does require that we desire cooperative relationships more than we desire competitive victory. If what we want *most* is superiority over others, our very real (but practically irrelevant) desire to have cooperative relationships will not come to fruition. On the other hand, if what we *desire* most is to cooperate with others, even our competitive striving will serve cooperative goals that allow us to get along with others.

From Family to Global Community

The scope of this book has been the family. Families are our first real community, and therefore our experiences as children set the tone for how we relate to non-familial communities. Our relationships with parents and caregivers helps us to know how to relate to authority figures: how to solicit care from those more skilled and resourced, and— hopefully— how to differentiate ourselves as individuals from the dominance hierarchy in which we exist. Our relationships with siblings help us to know how to relate to peers: how to play, problem solve, stick up for ourselves, and compromise. Our relationships with grandparents and older relatives help us to orient ourselves to the larger stories in which we live: how to learn from the mistakes of those we respect, how to grow old, and how to build a legacy.

In light of that, consider the impact of family dynamics. If a family strives horizontally, they set a precedent of cooperation that will leak out into friendships, school classrooms, college campuses, businesses, places of worship, neighborhoods, and politics. If — conversely — families inculcate vertical striving, they set a precedent of competition that will bleed out into all these same areas of life.

Cooperation in families isn't just about the nuclear family. It's about the *global* family.

What have competitive goals cost us? The more minuscule costs are failure to enjoy pleasant moments, overall increase in stress level, and constricted life activities. If we look closer, we find mental health diagnoses, lost friendships, social isolation, familial estrangement, hostile business activities, and petty crimes. When we allow a global view, we see the more harrowing costs: interpersonal violence, war, genocide, prejudices of every imaginable kind, political gridlock, violation of basic human rights.

The human desire to exert superiority *over* others has accounted for countless deaths, miseries, injustices, and missed opportunities. Contrarily, when human beings have joined together to strive away from inevitable feelings of inferiority and towards superiority *for/with* others, we have accomplished feats of almost unimaginable grandeur.

Diseases that even one hundred years ago were an existential threat to entire countries or continents have been functionally eradicated. Rates of extreme poverty dropped by almost half between the year 2000 and 2012, a rate of decrease unprecedented in the course of human history. Global life expectancy has risen, worldwide violence has decreased, and true luxuries (e.g., electricity, plumbing and septic systems, high-speed Internet access, etc.) are so readily available and cheap for most of the world that we now hardly notice that we have them.

If we were to study the histories of these positive changes, would we find that their source was a competitive goal? Would we discover that these feats were accomplished through the dominance of an individual or group over another? Would we find politicians, researchers, businesses, and systems solely invested in "winning" at any cost? Or rather, would we find that cooperation with others for the good of communities was what was desired *most*, even if accompanied by desire for competitive gain?

Certainly, we have more work to do. The current political climate in the United States insists that it is virtuous to hold "others" in contempt and overlook our faults, or the faults of those we deem "insiders." Nationalism[80] is on the rise, as are open expressions of prejudice from both conservative and liberal crowds. Some countries, including the United States, ignore the cooperative aspirations of international law when it might allow us a "leg up" on other nations. Governments afraid of losing power develop invasive surveillance infrastructures to hedge their bets against potential threats, even if it means violating their citizens' basic and previously-agreed-upon rights to privacy and autonomy.

This can all be quite overwhelming for any global citizen. We ask ourselves: "What can I do about the surveillance state? What can I do about conflict and prejudice in the Middle East? What can I do about homophobia, climate change, or fiscal irresponsibility in government?" Our answers to these questions are real and accessible, but often dissatisfying and disempowering.

We can carpool to reduce greenhouse gas emissions, but it feels like a drop in the bucket, or— perhaps more accurately— an ocean.

We can speak out against racism on social media. But then — of course — our post is mostly seen by people who agree with us, and if it *is* seen by someone who doesn't, they mostly likely scroll past what we've written, or write us off as naive or over-dramatic.

We can change our privacy settings on our Internet

80 A geopolitical expression of vertical striving: "Our nation is better than yours/theirs!"

browser, but — c'mon, who are we kidding? What kinds of surveillance are we under that we don't even know about?

We (if we live in the United States) can cast a vote in an election, but we're one in 325 million — does anyone really care what we think or want?[81]

There is something that we can do, something that has an enormous impact on communities small and large: *we can develop cooperative relationships within our families.*

What impact could one family have? Let us imagine.

At home, parents seek to win cooperation from their children rather than overpowering them. Chores are seen as a group challenge that must be managed by the whole family, rather than a set of requirements that come down from on high. Children are treated with respect and as if they have something to offer, which significantly reduces the intensity of their inferiority feelings. This, in turn, reduces their compensation through misbehavior.

Kids go to school in pleasant moods and armed with cooperative problem-solving tools, allowing them to be helpful and kind to their fellow students, rather than one-upping them through force, usury, or show. The whole classroom benefits, leading to improved behavior from all the students, improving the teacher's mood and ability to teach effectively.

---

81 By no means do I mean to diminish the importance of these actions, nor would I discourage anyone from engaging in them. On the contrary, I only wish to be honest about our common experience: these actions feel minimal, and rarely are we satisfied by the scope of our impact.

Students perform better on tests, leading to improved confidence and reduced feelings of inferiority, for which they would have — by virtue of their humanity — had to compensate. Parents, meanwhile, attend to their work free of the intense frustration of power struggle with children or each other. This leaves them graciously free of the need to compensate through work-related activities. They are empowered to be kind and cooperative with co-workers, improving the mood— and thereby, the productivity— of their workspace. Product or service quality improves, and prices drop even as profits increase. Solutions are discovered collaboratively, optimally utilizing *all* the strengths within the team instead of favoring a few and ignoring the rest. Due to improved problem-solving, confidence also increases, freeing the workplace of unnecessary compensations for feelings of inferiority [82] (e.g., failure to take meaningful risks, or insistence on taking unwise risks to "prove" oneself). These places of business, in turn, engage and collaborate with other businesses, having an indisputably positive impact on the local community.

The children, upon getting home from school, practice cooperation among themselves. Siblings solve problems together — however imperfectly —, learn from the pain of losing temporary friendship as a result of treating another with disrespect, and find ways to support one another. As

82 E.g., failure to take meaningful risks, or insistence on taking unwise risks to "prove" oneself.

Potential Impacts of Family Life

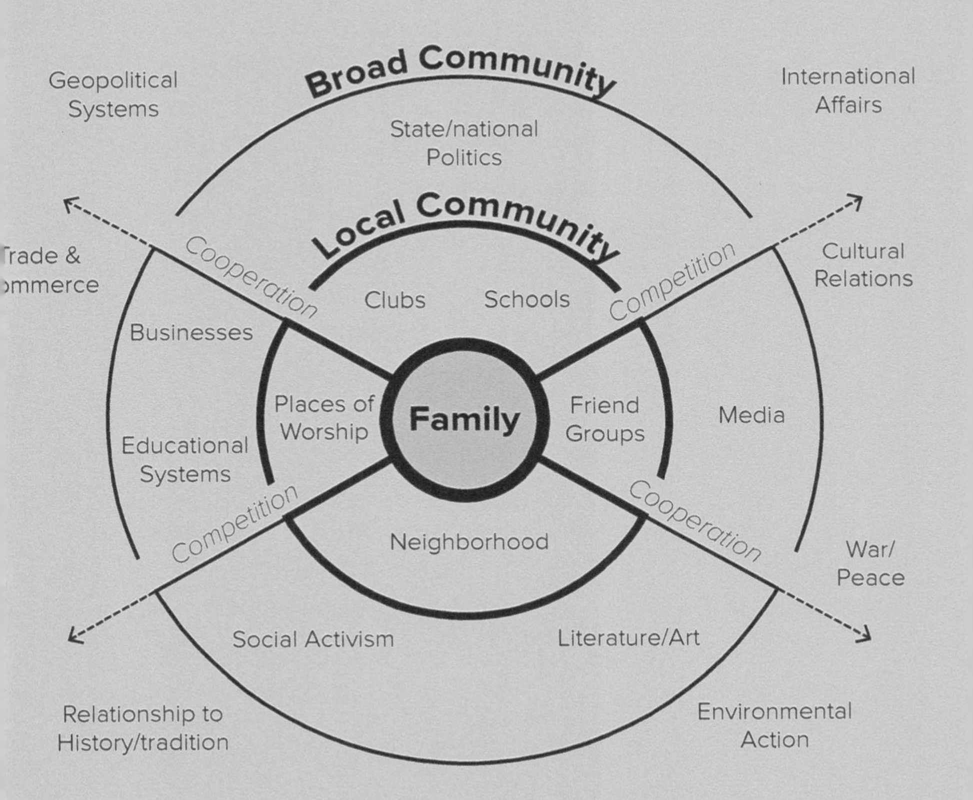

Global Community

they grow, they treat their friends in the same way, blessing an entire group of young people with kindness and respect, significantly reducing feelings of inferiority among the group. This in turn blesses numerous families with at least one member who isn't driven to compensate inappropriately.

Imagine that ten families lived like this. Or one hundred. A thousand? Ten thousand?

Imagine what it would be like if you lived in a world full of people who wanted to work *with* you, rather than defeat you in competition.

- *What defenses could you leave behind?*
- *What risks might you be encouraged to take?*
- *What wisdom would you finally develop?*
- *What bad habits could you abandon?*
- *How much more valued would you feel?*

Imagine if our world were full of people who— from an early age— learned that they have something to offer, rather than feeling that the world sits in opposition to their needs being met.

- *What conflicts could be avoided?*
- *What wars would we avoid, both global and local?*
- *What drug epidemics could we stop before they started?*

Perhaps you think that I'm overstating the case. You might say to yourself "There's no way that cooperation in a nuclear family can have that kind of impact." But my experience as a clinician and as a human being tells me that I'm not. I will shamelessly adapt an oft-quoted one-liner from my evangelical heritage: *it is not that cooperation has been tried and found wanting, but that it has not been tried at all.*

Act as if cooperative goals can reign supreme in your life, and in the life of your family. Act as if it were imperative that you and your family orient away from competitive striving and towards cooperation. Act as if it mattered that you do it, and that you do it with urgency.

I say to you with unfettered confidence that *you will not be disappointed with the results: For you. For your family. And for the world.*

Acknowledgments

Paul Rasmussen: Without your teaching, I would not have found Alfred Adler or learned to love him. From you, I learned how people behave and change. That understanding has allowed me to be empathetic and cooperative. Your impact on my personal and professional life is immeasurable.

Erin Hahn: Thank you for giving me a chance to be over-zealous, curious, and ambitious in your lab in the Summer of 2007. More importantly, thanks for your ongoing friendship. You have helped me to know that what I do matters. You are an indelible part of this book.

Frank & Kathy Walton: Your lives are a picture of horizontal striving. You don't just teach theory, you live it. Your message to me — a counselor in training — was "We like you, we believe in you, you matter, you belong, and get your ass in gear because we need you to lend a hand." I can't imagine a more dignifying and precious message.

Lindsay Hill: You're one of a few who have permitted me to "nerd out" about Adler and my fantastical ideas of writing a book. It's hard to imagine how I could have finished this project without your undying support and genuine excitement.

Wes Wingett: You are a diligent and generous model of cooperative striving. You have every reason to condescend to others: you are bright, you are likable, you are kind, and you are a true master in your field. Yet, you put all of that to use for the well-being of others.

The South Carolina Society of Adlerian Psychology: Thank you for being a place I belong, where my youth was never cause for contempt or condescension. Thank you for letting me teach, and for letting me enjoy your strengths.

Kelly Shimmel, David Newell, & John Carenen: Thank you for critical eyes to a messy manuscript, even as folks who aren't in the mental health field. This book will undoubtedly be of better help to others because of your contributions.

David Shimmel: Thank you for your committed friendship, and your unparalleled aesthetic sensibilities to the artwork, layout, and design of the book. My readers would have received a poorly-bound, Xerox'd pamphlet without your help.

Jessie, Truman, & Ruby: Thank you for being smiling faces when your depressive, head-in-the-clouds husband/father comes home, for loaning me to my word processor for long hours, and for being a family that works with me to make and maintain cooperative goals, for ourselves and for the world.

References

Abramson, Z. (2007). Adlerian family and couples therapy. Journal of Individual Psychology, 63, 371-386.

Adler, A. (1938). Social Interest: A Challenge to Mankind. London, UK: Faber & Faber.

Chalmers, T. (1846). The Expulsive Power of a New Affection In *Sermons and Discourses* (New York: R. Carter).

Dreikurs, R. (1964). Democratic and Autocratic Child Rearing In Jenkins, H. (Ed.) *The Children's Culture Reader*. p. 504. New York, NY: New York University Press.

Gottman, J. M. (1994). What Predicts Divorce? The Relationship Between Marital Processes and Marital Outcomes. Hillsdale, NJ: Lawrence Erlbaum Associates.

Livingstone, R. W. (1954). On Education: The Future in Education and Eeducation for a World Adrift. (Cambridge, UK: Cambridge).

Rasmussen, P. R. (2010). *The Quest to Feel Good*. Abingdon, UK: Routledge.

Shurr, A., & Ritov, I. (2016). Winning a competition Predicts Dishonest Behavior. *Proceedings of the National Academy of Sciences*, 113(7), 1754-1759.

UNESCO (2017). *Reading the Past, Writing the Ffuture: Fifty Years of Promoting Literacy*. Paris, UNESCO. pp. 21–23, 26.

Walton, F. X. (1998). Use of the Most Memorable Observation as a Technique for Understanding Choice of Parenting Style. *Journal of Individual Psychology*, 54 (4)

Index

A

B

C

D

E

F

G

H

I

J

K

L

M

O

P

Q

R

S

T

U

V

W

Y

Additional Reviews

What a gift this book is to anyone who reads it, and a gift to those in the lives of those readers. Rarely does a book bring meaningful topics together so clearly and with such accessibility. It is our inability to cooperate with one another that activates our greatest insecurities, discomforts and emotional pains and that ignites our worst demons. It will only be through our ability to live cooperatively that we humans will resolve our most significant challenges, fulfill our desires for safety and validation and realize our most virtuous potentials. The opportunity to cooperate begins at the most basic unit of human engagement, the family, and these experiences set the foundation for cooperation within the whole of humanity. Calvin Armerding has captured in beautiful prose the challenges we face and opportunities we have for meeting our greatest challenge. This is a "must read."

-Paul Rasmussen, Ph.D., DNASAP; Psychologist, WJB Dorn Veteran's Affairs Medical Center, Columbia, SC, USA; Author of The Quest to Feel Good

The Cooperative Family can truly help individuals, couples, families, and communities attain higher levels of cooperation and connection. Armerding offers a compelling and modern interpretation of Alfred Adler's theory-- in an easy to read format. I will recommend this book to all of my students, supervisees, and clients.

Jon Sperry, Ph.D., Assoc. Professor of Clinical Mental Health Counseling, Lynn University; Co-Editor, Journal of Individual Psychology

"A must read book for all parents and clinicians working with families. With relatable case studies and scripts from counselling sessions, theory becomes practical advice for co-operative living within families and the community at-large. A most hopeful book for improving oneself and all humanity."

-Alyson Schafer, MA; Author of Ain't Misbehavin' and The Good Mom Myth

This is a precise examination of the extensive impact that an underdeveloped sense of cooperation has upon relationships. Calvin provides specific and powerful illustrations of how we can overcome this debilitating liability in daily life. The work is a gift to therapists, parents, and couples.

-Francis X. Walton, Ph.D.; Faculty member, International Committee for Adlerian Summer Schools and Institutes; Former President, North American Society of Adlerian Psychology